Win-Win Labor-Management Collaboration In Education

Breakthrough Practices to Benefit Students, Teachers, and Administrators

Researched and Authored by LINDA KABOOLIAN

With PAUL SUTHERLAND

Public Sector Labor Management Program, Taubman Center for State and Local Government

John F. Kennedy School of Government, Harvard University

Research Sponsors: The Barr Foundation, The Jessie B. Cox Charitable Trust

RENNIE CENTER
for Education Research & Policy

Edited and Produced by the Rennie Center for Education Research & Policy

S. PAUL REVILLE, Executive Director

JENNIFER CANDON, Assistant Director

CELINE COGGINS, Research Director

EDUCATION WEEK PRESS

To order copies of this book,
Telephone: (800) 788-5692
Online: http://www.edweek.org/go/products
Or write: Education Week Press
6935 Arlington Road, Suite 100
Bethesda, MD 20814

Visit us on the Web at edweek.org.

Subscriptions to *Education Week* are available at:
edweek.org/offer or by calling (800) 728-2790

Also from EDUCATION WEEK PRESS:

*The Last Word: The Best Commentary and Controversy
in American Education* (co-published with Jossey-Bass)

Cutting Through the Hype: A Taxpayer's Guide To School Reforms

Lessons of a Century: A Nation's Schools Come of Age

Living the Legacy: Education Week *marks the 50th anniversary
of the* Brown *v.* Board of Education of Topeka *decision*

*Creating the Capacity for Change: How and Why Governors and Legislatures
Are Opening a New-Schools Sector in Public Education*

Building Bridges With the Press: A Guide for Educators

*Miles To Go ... Reflections on Mid-Course Corrections
For Standards-Based Reform*

Preface

We believe that if the ultimate goal of education reform – *improving students' educational opportunities and achievement* — is to be met, adult professional relationships in the field must be fundamentally transformed.

Standards-based reform has introduced significant accountability into the public education sector. Student learning now matters more deeply than ever before. Students are held accountable for achieving high learning standards while adults are increasingly being held responsible for creating opportunities for all students to learn. This is a fundamental change with profound implications. If student learning is truly to be central in the field of education, then the nature of professional relationships between adults in education must be significantly strengthened.

Prominent among these implications is the necessity to place student learning at the center of the educational enterprise and to organize adult professional relationships in ways that maximize student learning. Increasingly, schools and school systems will be judged by their effectiveness at improving student learning and meeting educational standards. The new requirements of standards-based education, coupled with the increasing introduction of competition to traditional public providers, makes it imperative that the professionals in mainstream public schools find new, more effective ways of working together to improve student achievement. If we are to retain the current generation of new teachers, who echo this demand for strengthened professional relationships, this shift becomes an even greater priority. The transformation of adult relationships within the public education sector is not only a matter of fairness to students, but it may be a matter of survival for the industry.

In response to this challenge, the Rennie Center for Education Research & Policy has embarked on a multi-year effort involving research and public convening that seeks to transform district-level, professional relationships between teachers' unions, superintendents, and school boards in order to improve student learning. The production of this innovative practices handbook, in partnership with the book's researchers and authors—Linda Kaboolian and Paul Sutherland — is one component of our work on the topic of labor-management relations. We believe that by seeking innovative ways for educational leaders to collaborate, the institution of public education will be better able to maintain and build public confidence and will be equipped to meet the increasingly stringent demands for accountability amidst heightened competition. For this reason, the Rennie Center's work focuses on developing frameworks, opportunities, and reference tools to support educational leaders as they work together to establish new working relationships that put

student achievement at the center of the educational enterprise.

The Rennie Center is initiating this effort in hopes that labor and school management can break out of the current confines of entrenched collective-bargaining arrangements and experiment with creative, developmental practices that will enable student achievement. In many cases, labor leaders, superintendents, and school board members have expressed their desire to transform the current status of labor-management relations and expand student-centered decision-making. However, many of these same educational leaders say they do not know how to initiate the transition, citing the need for guidance and information about innovative practices and strategies for working together. There are no easy answers or quick fixes that dramatically improve student achievement, let alone reform the education industry by improving the current state of labor-management relations. However, addressing these challenges must be directly at the heart of any strategy to realize our national aspirations of providing all children with a high-quality education.

S. Paul Reville, Executive Director
Rennie Center for Education Research & Policy

Introduction

This "best practices" handbook provides a catalogue of innovative labor-management practices in public education for educational practitioners who are engaged in labor-management relations and collective bargaining.

Our primary focus is to identify practices that promote student-centered decision-making, thus enabling educational leaders to overcome obstacles to improved student achievement and performance of the system. This desk reference offers a national review of pathbreaking collective-bargaining agreements and related contract provisions that have led to promising new professional practices and a sharpened adult focus on student achievement. By communicating best practices in an accessible and understandable manner, we seek to respond to the field's demand for information and guidance. This handbook has relevance and value for a wide audience, including: school board members, superintendents, union leaders, these groups' lawyers, as well as other individuals who may be engaged in negotiations or otherwise seeking to improve labor relations.

We hope that the innovations described here will raise the field's expectations for what can be accomplished and educational leaders' understanding about ways of working together to improve student achievement. Innovative practices catalogued in this handbook are not prescriptions for change, but rather, possible models for simultaneously satisfying the institutional needs of negotiating parties and for improving student achievement. While the descriptions and contract language cited in this handbook will not tell us what is happening on the ground as a result of these provisions, we hope that, in combination with the descriptions, discussions and resources offered at the end of each section, these examples could inspire educational leaders, open dialogue and stimulate the thinking of teachers, their unions, and school district leaders.

REFORM AS A COLLABORATIVE PROCESS

Adversarial relationships between teachers and school management significantly impede change efforts required to improve student achievement. Adversity is expensive and hinders a clear focus on students, using up resources—money, time, energy, and leadership attention—which could be put to better use.

Research supports the premise that collaborative work is essential to education reform. While policymakers and managers can adopt standards of practice, they cannot mandate actions in classrooms where instruction takes place.[1] In order to change instructional procedure, teachers must be active participants in the design and implementation of new practices.[2] For example, a study of Maryland school districts that compared low-performing schools against successful schools found that:

Student achievement is likely to be greatest

where teachers and administrators work together, in small groups and school-wide, to identify sources of student success and then struggle collectively to implement school improvement.[3]

Research done in conjunction with whole-school-reform models also demonstrates the connection between collaboration and improved outcomes.[4] Links between increased student achievement and collaborative, adult problem-solving may be strongest in schools with high concentrations of poor students[5]—a finding with important implications for closing the achievement gap.

Distributed leadership—the leadership of multiple individuals, rather than one person—strengthens an organization by increasing its capacity to engage in, respond to and institutionalize constructive change.[6] Indeed, research shows that student achievement is more likely to improve when leadership focused on educational quality is distributed across the school community and among stakeholder groups.[7]

As demonstrated by examples within this handbook, the union plays an important role as an institutional actor in promoting distributed leadership. Employee participation in problem solving is most likely to result in improved organizational performance, if the union is supportive of the effort and involved in the design and governance of the participation mechanism.[8] Changes in practices require the consent of all parties. As a result, where there is a collective-bargaining agreement, only the most superficial types of participation would be possible, if the union were not a partner.

A NEW VISION OF REFORM

Public education is in a period of dynamic change and is under intense scrutiny due to the increased focus on accountability. The exclusive franchise that school districts once had is facing competitive challenge by charters and vouchers. With this increased emphasis on student performance and the competitive pressure of choice, the current education delivery system as we know it is at risk. Teachers, administrators, school board members, parents, and many community members feel they have a stake in the success of their public schools. These stakeholders, with a common interest in preserving public education, can work together to devise new strategies for success.[9]

More than threats to the system make this work possible. Teachers, administrators, and school boards share a genuine concern about children and closing the achievement gap between high and lower-performing student groups. However, not surprisingly, changes required to address these problems breed conflict. This conflict between adults in public school systems must be overcome and replaced with a more constructive way of working together to better serve students.

Superintendents and school boards are beginning to see the wisdom in working with other stakeholders, particularly unions, on education reform. Superintendents have a lot at stake and are often the first affected by accountability.

Former urban superintendents gave their peers the following advice at a recent colloquium regarding working with unions on education reform:

- Encourage collaboration around the 'main thing'—student achievement. Ideally, the contract becomes a living document that adjusts and changes continually as understanding of student achievement evolves.
- Make the contract the instrument for advancing student learning. If it isn't in the contract, it's not really the main thing.
- Think of negotiating as a problem-solving mechanism, not a source of conflict. Ideally it should be a perpetual tool for problem-solving.
- Unions have an interest in good schools, too.
- Keep up to speed on what's happening with union reform. Some of the most progressive ideas about how to advance the learning are coming from union leaders themselves.[10]

Unions, too, recognize the significant institutional challenges they face and the consequent need to adopt new ways of working with school leaders.[11] Increasingly, unions must respond to a changing membership with different demands. The generation whose loyalty was won in the fight for professional wage scales is retiring out of the system. New teachers want a more professional and issues-linked relationship with their union, and research suggests that they rank salary considerably lower in preference to other professional concerns, including: engaging with supportive administrators, collaborating with highly motivated and effective professional colleagues, and working in mission-driven schools that share their teaching philosophies.[12] As a result, unions are now called on to provide help with instructional practice, continuous professional education, and meeting requirements of an increasingly regulated profession.

Contrary to a traditional view of unions as "reform blockers," teachers' unions have proven to be important institutional education reform partners in many locations and have increasingly engaged in "value-added unionism"—a practice of using institutional capacity to further the success of their districts, while protecting their members' interests.

We believe that both union leaders and school managers must adopt a new vision of labor relations that puts student achievement at the center of the collective-bargaining process. In so doing, negotiating parties must acknowledge that working together in different ways will entail changes in behavior on both sides. Both school managers and teachers' unions have a vested interest in seeing their enterprises succeed and in ensuring that public education does not erode. The practices and contract language in this handbook document the positive contribution that unions and school managers, through collaboration, can provide to education reform efforts.

COLLECTIVE BARGAINING: A TOOL FOR PROGRESS

This handbook focuses on identifying innovative working relationships that place student learning at the center of the educational enterprise. While this book is not about collective bargaining specifically, we recognize collective bargaining as a tool—an instrument that structures relationships, describes roles, protects rights, sets expectations and limits, while creating the possibility for change. The end product of collective bargaining—the district contract— defines teachers' work practices and, through codification, often institutionalizes innovative ways of working together. The collective-bargaining process reflects the tone of labor-management relations and parties' attitudes toward student-centered decision-making. To quote one former urban superintendent,

> "…The contract is the union's 'sacred text.' If it isn't in the contract, it isn't important."[13]

Too often, collective-bargaining agreements embody the cumulative scar tissue of brutal battles between negotiating parties in their pursuit of autonomy and control. Contracts resulting from adversarial relationships are thick with restrictive work rules, detailed descriptions of when they apply, and numerous exceptions. The focus is on the needs of adults rather than the improvement of student learning. In most contracts, labor and school management have established a narrow relationship in which student achievement is largely irrelevant, severely limiting their capacity to reorganize for expanded productivity.

The contract serves as the framework around which collaboration is possible and from which new ways of working together can be institutionalized. In some instances, negotiating parties are able to "work things out" because positive, trusting relationships develop at the leadership level. However, these positive relationships between leaders do not always carry over to the school level, where further implementation challenges may arise. The innovative practices cited in this handbook are notable because they represent a departure from the traditional goals and strategies embodied in collective bargaining. Explicitly student-focused, these practices represent a transformation in the structure of relationship between the parties, institutionalizing new ways of working together at the district and school levels. In these examples, leaders' strong relationships may have been the catalyst initiating collaboration, but the resulting collective-bargaining agreement (as embodied in contract language) reflects the leaders' collaborative spirit and seeks to actively transform the structural relationships between school-level participants.

Examples of innovative collective-bargaining practices and contract language in this handbook suggest something more than relationship building is occurring. In particular — student achievement is recognized as important to both parties, as well as to students, parents, and taxpayers. As a result, negotiating parties express a growing willingness to look beyond the current ways of doing things and to experiment with new working relationships. Innovations embody openness to the possibility that the other side has good ideas and flexibility, rather than positional rigidity, about how one's interests are served.

CATALYSTS & IMPEDIMENTS TO COLLABORATION & INNOVATION

The districts cited in this handbook are not so unique that replicating their collaborative work would be impossible. Districts represent a range of sizes, including the largest urban districts, suburban counties, and small towns. Their populations are diverse and often impoverished but not always so. No one element characterizes these districts except that some stakeholder, internal or external to the system, wanted and believed that by working together the parties could produce better student outcomes.

Catalysts driving collaboration differ. In some cases, a superintendent and union leader build on a strong personal working relationship. In other instances, one leader reaches out to an adversary. External stakeholders also play a role in leading the transformation of labor-management relations. For instance, in Boston, the business community intervened at a moment of impasse. In other districts, foundations work with individual school systems to support their tentative steps, or they become involved at a more systemic level by supporting leadership-training programs aimed at fostering collaboration on student achievement. District networks like the Teacher Union Reform Network have also helped to spark and support innovation.[14] National unions can support locals with technical assistance and resources if they express interest in collaborating with administrators; however, national bodies cannot require this involvement since locals are permitted to retain autonomy from the national union and pursue divergent courses. These different impetuses demonstrate that innovation can occur in a range of environs and under diverse circumstances.

Innovation requires that the leaders of each stakeholder group be willing and able to bring their own constituents along the politically treacherous path of change. Each party must invest in the development of its constituency's technical, political, and educational capacities because new skills may be required within a collaborative environment. Even in districts where the desire for collaboration and innovation exists, the "work of change" requires political skills to gain stakeholder support. Unions and school boards are political organizations, and differences will exist between leaders' and members' perceptions about the need for and value of change. As one superintendent put it:

> "Leaders and members are different constituencies. Often the leader is out ahead of members on key educational issues."[15]

Union leaders and school district managers are more likely to be open to collaboration than their constituents. The reform environment looks different to leaders who travel to national conventions or who participate in professional networks outside their home districts. These leaders will hear the early warnings that change is necessary. They will learn about pilot projects and experiments in other districts. Their repertoire of strategies will expand as they meet and learn from peers, and they will encounter resources to cope with the new challenges that they face. Constituents who rarely experience horizon-broadening opportunities will need convincing that new ways of doing business will be worth the effort and pain.

Despite their broader exposure to the benefits of collaboration, both school district managers and union leaders face additional disincentives to work together. The following issues have been cited as possible impediments to overcome:

- **Perceived violation of fair representation.**
  Unions may have a more difficult time with collaboration if working with management appears to violate legal standards for union action. In exchange for the right to exclusively represent their members, unions are required to fulfill their obligations to represent and advocate for *all* members, even the bad actors.[16]

- **Traditional conceptions of unions' function.**
  Members may have traditional notions about a union's function, which is limited to a narrow focus on wages, hours, and working conditions. As teachers' unions have begun to expand their repertoire and engage management around issues of professional practice, governance, and education reform, many of their members worry that they abandon economic and representational issues. The fallacy in this thinking is the assumption that advocacy over economic and representational issues is incompatible with collaborative work relating to education reform.

- **History of poor labor-management relations.**
  The union and district's relationship history may also be an obstacle to effective collaboration. Strikes that occurred years in the past and under the leadership of long retired superintendents and school board members may still influence members of the teachers' union. It may be difficult for a superintendent with 18 months tenure in a district to realize that his or her interaction with different constituents may be impacted by distrust sown years ago.[17] Trust between people is more easily restored than trust between institutions.

- **Tension caused by budgetary constraints.**
  External factors such as fiscal tightening may pose additional obstacles to collaboration if conditions threaten parties' interests. Many people see layoffs, or even the threat of layoffs, to be "the third rail" of collaboration, causing significant stress in stakeholder relationships. Trends in many states toward late budget resolution exacerbate these challenges and function to alienate even the most faithful educators who might be engaged in collaboration.

- **Opposition to change and innovation.** All stakeholder groups—unions, school managers, school boards, and community members—have individual leaders and members who are resistant to new ways of doing things or working together. These individuals may be more comfortable with the existing status than risking an unknown scenario. Additionally, in many instances, there may be little incentive to change working arrangements that are beneficial to adult professionals.

- **Managerial accountability pressures.**
  Management faces greater accountability pressures, and thus may be less willing to engage in reforms that limit central office prerogatives. The expectation of many school boards is that a superintendent, as a district's chief executive

officer, is expected to be decisive and to make things happen.

- **Anti-union sentiment.** Superintendents may also have to deal with their constituents' negative reaction to collaboration with the teachers' union. School board members, mayors, and the news media might be anti-union, seeing little value in the parties working together. Rather than involving unions in reform efforts, these players may prefer that unions are further constrained or that their existence is eliminated altogether. Collaborative work may be seen as an undesirable "soft" technique, if stakeholders believe that hard choices and decisive action are required. In this environment, administrators who advocate for collaboration may be criticized or marginalized.

- **Difficulty reversing trend of union exclusion.** When hiring new superintendents, school board members rarely discuss if or how teachers' unions will be involved in reform efforts. While unions may have their supporters on school boards, the important issue of union inclusion often remains unaddressed. Even in districts with a history of successful collaboration, this course can be negatively impacted if a new superintendent is hired who is either unaware or inimical to existing working relationships.

In spite of these impediments, many leaders have found ways to "break through" conventional barriers. Their efforts are documented in this book.

FORMS OF COLLABORATION AND INNOVATION

Collaborative work between teachers' unions and administrators takes a variety of forms. The specific context of a situation will influence the process, scope, and direction of innovative developments. Not every innovative practice is well suited to every district. State laws governing unionization, collective bargaining, and education reform vary considerably—in some cases, impeding innovation and in other instances facilitating it.

The form of innovative working relationships can vary. Some relationships are formalized in contracts, while others are established through Memoranda of Understanding or side agreements. Others exist for years without being formally codified in writing. There are advantages and disadvantages to each form. The existence of contract language creates enforceable rights and responsibilities, which can continue even if party leadership changes. However, contract language requires ratification, which may be too high a hurdle for an experimental practice. Productive collaborative relationships may also continue with no formal agreement, incorporating new ways of working together in everyday interactions and delegating problem-solving and innovation to joint committees at the school levels.

The innovations listed here exist on a continuum of complexity and may take a number of different forms. For example, innovations involving pay for performance may require a different type of collaboration than contract overrides. Similarly, peer assistance practices may differ depending upon the circumstances of their implementation—in some instances involving occasional interaction between a mentor and new teacher, while in other cases, entailing elaborate programs governed by a joint labor-management committee. Not all innovations can be equated in terms of the amount of work required for implementation or their possible effect on student achievement. Also, it is worth noting that in several cases, districts have adopted multiple innovations that are mutually reinforcing when they occur in a cluster.[18] The range in scope and complexity of innovative practices is reflected within this handbook's discussion.

IMPACT ON STUDENT ACHIEVEMENT

This handbook does not evaluate the effect that specific innovative practices have had on student achievement; such analysis is beyond the scope of this work. However, if a specific district's practice has been evaluated, we cite this research, as well as evidence justifying the value of these innovations to student achievement. Collaboration and the transformation of working relations often affect intermediary processes—such as collaboration among educators, district culture, and teacher practice—rather than impacting student learning in a directly quantifiable way. For this reason, there is not a large amount of research documenting the clear link between strengthened labor relations and improved student achievement. Intuitively, the connection is clear — collaborative, student-centered decision-making is more likely to result in student gains than adherence to a set of confrontational, adult-focused interactions.

The union's involvement is both directly and indirectly connected to the success of a school or district. Directly, union-management relations determine the way organizational resources will be used in pursuit of organizational goals. Because teacher salaries comprise the bulk of education spending, collective-bargaining agreements outline a large percentage of a district's budget. Less directly, the tenor of labor management relationships will play a large role in determining the value that can be created by available resources and the extent to which more satisfying professional jobs can be created. High-trust, participatory relationships have been shown to enhance organizational effectiveness. Low-trust, conflict-ridden relationships experience attendant costs associated with conflict mediation, absenteeism, and high turnover.[19]

CHALLENGES OF IDENTIFYING INNOVATION

Knowledgeable observers can cite examples where a discrepancy exists between contract language and practice on the ground. These discrepancies may run in both directions—in some cases, innovative contract language does not translate into innovative practice, and, in other instances, innovative practice is not codified within the contract. There are a number of reasons why a discrepancy may occur. Good intentions expressed during contract negotiations may not translate into action, if those responsible for implementation lack requisite skills, resources and/or good will. In other cases, district-wide policy decisions may not represent appropriate strategies for all schools. Alternatively, innovations may arise indigenously at the school level, but may not be sufficiently developed or supported to be institutionalized on a district-wide level. In other instances, parties resist codifying new practices and relationships because informality preserves each side's ability to withdraw unilaterally from the practice. Sometimes, leaders choose not to formally change a contract, so that they can work toward implementing an innovation without need to seek formal authorization from their constituents.

Innovations contained within this text have been verified through discussions with both labor and management representatives and scrutinized in regards to whether innovative agreements have actually been implemented. However, observers may vary in their perceptions of these innovations and the extent to which they have been actualized. We value these differences in perception as they represent important insights that can contribute to creative problem-solving.

CLASSIFICATION OF INNOVATIVE PRACTICES

Arguably, there were many ways to classify each innovation, and the boundaries between many innovations are judgment calls. While some of the topics covered here seem traditional, both the process of negotiating them and the substance of new provisions challenge conventional roles and relationships between the contracting parties. In addition, these innovations address important problems, clustered into five areas of activity, which are described below:

BARGAINING METHODS AND NEW FORMS OF AGREEMENTS.

The negotiations process, as well as the content and form of the agreements, have changed. Student achievement is explicitly addressed as the parties' purpose. Procedures for altering contract components are more flexible and less cumbersome. Contracts are shrinking from encyclopedia volumes filled with regulations and innumerable exceptions to "thin" contracts that set some district-wide standards but allow most conditions, particularly work rules, to be negotiated at the school site level. Parties attempt to find terms that provide the maximum value for each side rather than assuming "winner takes all" postures. In this section, we describe:

- Interest-based bargaining
- Salary benchmarking
- Thin contracts
- Waivers and override procedures
- Living contracts
- Language on student achievement

IMPROVING THE QUALITY OF TEACHING AND TEACHERS.

Student achievement is premised on: hiring good teachers, assigning these teachers where they are needed, providing them with the necessary skills and support, assuring that their time is used in sufficient quantity on teaching, competently assessing teaching performance, intervening when teachers falter, efficiently removing those who should not be teaching, and rewarding effective efforts.

Professional development represents a constellation of practices, which not only include preparing new teachers and upgrading the skill set of the existing teaching force, but also encompasses the creation of internal professional job ladders for teachers thus recognizing teaching prowess and working to increase teacher retention. In this section, we describe:

- Teacher hiring, assignment, and transfer policies
- Professional development of new and continuing teachers
- Peer review and assistance
- Pay for performance
- Evaluations by families and students

DEVOLVING AND DEREGULATING SCHOOLS.

The process of devolving and deregulating schools is premised on the theory that the people closest to students—teachers, building administrators, and parents—will make decisions that are more responsive to student needs than those made by central office bureaucrats. The goal of these innovations is to shift administrative control from the district level to the building level. Often this entails breaking large schools into smaller units with special foci or services. Additionally, there is reduced emphasis on district-wide standardization of schools and increased variation in whole school design, possibly including the establishment of charters. In this section, we describe:

- Site-based management
- High-autonomy schools
- Small learning communities

IMPROVING LOW-PERFORMING SCHOOLS.

This set of innovations involves multi-stakeholder intervention in low-performing schools. Prior to *No Child Left Behind Act* authorizations, federal regulations already required a multi-stakeholder process to devise

School Improvement Plans (SIP) for schools performing poorly on state assessment tests. Innovations noted in this section formalize SIP processes, explicitly stating the roles and responsibilities of each stakeholder group. More importantly, they recognize low performance as an urgent issue and liberalize or waive existing contract terms in order to focus on student achievement. In this section, we describe:

- Special districts
- School intervention processes
- Extending the school day and year

PARTNERING.

Recognizing that student achievement is a shared endeavor, these innovations engage stakeholders both inside and outside of the school system in order to expand resources, capture good ideas, and develop support and shared ownership over change processes and outcomes. Innovations exist on a continuum of formality. In some instances, they include informal, undocumented relationships between individual labor and administrative leaders, who are working together on mutually defined problems to find mutually satisfactory solutions. In other instances, partnerships involve very formal, institutionalized structures for stakeholder power sharing. In this section, we describe:

- Strategic partnerships
- Joint problem-solving
- External partnerships
- Cross-district consultation

ORGANIZATION OF THIS HANDBOOK

Innovative practices contained within this handbook were identified through a national scan and via contact with a variety of professional networks. Our search was aided by the two national teachers' unions, as well as organizations representing school boards, labor attorneys, and superintendents. During the course of our review, we found that a great deal of collaborative innovation exists and has been ongoing for many years. Because of the wide breadth of positive work being accomplished around the nation, we were unable to include all identified innovations in this handbook. To provide readers with a manageable foundation from which to draw inspiration and ideas, we selected a sampling of practices that best exemplified new ways of working together.

Readers are able to reference this handbook to read selectively about innovative practices. As described in the prior section, innovative practices have been organized and presented thematically under umbrella headers. Innovative practices are briefly defined, and their usefulness to improving student learning is noted. Problems that each innovative practice addresses are also clarified. For readers interested in learning more about how specific innovative practices evolved and were implemented, short district scenarios are reviewed. Pertinent information about each scenario's history, special circumstances, and participants is included. Additionally, so that readers can contact district leaders to learn more, contact information for relevant individuals is provided at the end of each section.

Many districts that have pursued innovative practices have documented these new working relations in their contract language, some of which we reference in this book. Contract language cited in this handbook is taken from current contracts, though there may have been different provisions in previous contracts. Some of these innovations have evolved over time and through experimentation. If readers are curious to learn more about the context behind an innovative practice and its related contract language, we encourage them to contact the district's union and administrative leaders.

CONCLUSION

We believe that the reshaping of working relationships in education is absolutely essential to student success and the success of reform. Across the nation, educators, school leaders, and policymakers cite the need to improve relationships among professionals in public education. There is widespread interest in the issue, but there is little documentation of strategies for addressing it. We have confidence that local leaders, if given the proper opportunity, facilitation, expertise, and support, will be able to make significant headway in redefining their professional relationships in ways that place student achievement at the center of adults' work in education. We hope that this reference guide contributes to a process of engendering, in the field, a vision of new, more flexible, and effective relationships that focus on improving student learning while providing educators with more gratifying, successful professional jobs.

FOOTNOTES

1. Elmore, R. (2002). "Hard Questions About Practice." *Beyond Instructional Leadership.* (5)22-25.

2. Stringfield, S. and Ross, S. (1997). "A Reflection at Mile Three of a Marathon." *School Effectiveness and School Improvement.* (March). 8(1)

3. Schafer, W.D.; Hultgren, F.; Hawley, W.D.; Abrams, A.L.; Seubert, C.C.; and Mazzoni, S. (No publication date). *Study of Higher Success and Lower Success Elementary Schools.* Available on the Maryland Assessment Archive at www.marces.org/mdarch/shell.asp?wtest=MSPAP.

4. Datnow, A. and Stringfield, S. (2000). Working Together for Reliable School Reform. *Journal of Education of Students Placed at Risk.* Vol.5(1&2).
5. Schafer, W.D.; Hultgren, F.; Hawley, W.D.; Abrams, A.L.; Seubert, C.C.; and Mazzoni, S. (No publication date). *Study of Higher Success and Lower Success Elementary Schools.* www.mdk12.org/process/benchmark/improve/

6. Spillane, J.P.; Halverson, R.; Diamond, J.B. (2001). Investigating School Leadership Practice: A Distributed Perspective. *Educational Researcher.* 30(3):23-28. Newmann, F., Wehlage, G. (1995). *Successful School Restructuring: A Report to the Public and Educations.* Madison, WI: University of Wisconsin Education Center.

7. Ibid.

8. Research on participatory schemes distinguishes between employee involvement programs where individual employees (or work teams) have the opportunity to make suggestions to improve productivity, quality and service and programs and programs where employees and their union representatives participate in strategic choices. Findings from research of these different types of programs make clear that the positive effects of participation are greater and longer lasting when unions as well as individual employees are involved and when the domain of discretion is expanded to include strategic issues.

9. See Sherif, M., et al. (1954). *Intergroup Conflict and Cooperation: The Robbers Cave Experiment.* Norman, OK: University of Oklahoma Press. This book is also available at: www.psychclassics.yorku.ca/Sherif/

10. Harvey, J. (2003). *The Urban Superintendent: Creating Great Schools While Surviving on the Job.* Council of Great City Schools. Page 27.

11. Kerchner, C.T.; Koppich, J.E.; and Weeres, J.G. (1997). *United Mind Workers: Unions and Teaching in the Knowledge Society.* San Francisco: Jossey-Bass.

12. Farkas, S.; Johnson, J.; Foleno, T. (2000) *A Sense of Calling: Who Teaches and Why.* Public Agenda.

13. Harvey, J. (2003). *The Urban Superintendent: Creating Great Schools While Surviving on the Job.* Council of Great City Schools. Page 27.

14. The American Federation of Teachers (AFT) established the Redesigning Schools to Raise Student Achievement network to support collaborative reform efforts at the local level. A group of local unions affiliated with both the AFT and the National Education Association founded the Teacher Union Reform Network (TURN).

15. Harvey, J. (2003). *The Urban Superintendent: Creating Great Schools While Surviving on the Job.* Council of Great City Schools. Page 27.

16. The Duty to Fair Representation requirement protects members who may not be in political favor with the union leadership, and it protects all members from union leaders colluding with management against the members. While unions do not strictly need to put their full weight behind every member, the penalties for failure to fairly represent a member are heavy. At the same time, union officers know that vigorous representation of members who do not carry their weight in the workplace can be a political liability. As much as members want their union to represent them, should they need it, they also resent doing the work of non-performing employees and do not want their union to spend financial and political resources protecting bad actors. As a result, union officers must exercise political savvy in working with administrators to improve student achievement.

17. This point is best illustrated by the experience of one urban district that sent its union and administrative leadership on a retreat. When asked to draw a time line of the relationship, the union leaders came back with details stretching back 25 years. The administrators described only the last two years.

18. the effects of clustered innovations in comparison to stand-alone innovations have been studied in detail by economists. Researchers have found that adopting work practice innovations in isolation has little or no effect on organizational outcomes. See, for example: Ichniowski, C., et al. 1997. The Effects of Human Resource Management Practices on Productivity. *American Economic Review.* 86 (6):291-313.

19. Norsworthy, J.R. and Zabala, C. (1985). Worker Attitudes, Worker Behavior and Productivity in the American Automobile Industry, 1959-1976. *Industrial and Labor Relations Review* 38:556.

Bargaining Methods
and New Forms
of Agreements

The collective-bargaining process is the most visible ritual and symbol of labor-management relationships in public education. Teachers had to fight long and hard for the right to organize and bargain. Consequently, adversity and mistrust have frequently clouded the relationship between labor and management from its beginning. The relationship did not improve with the expansion of the scope and power of teachers' unions since the 1960s. Even today, the legitimacy of teachers' unions is sometimes questioned, and unions exist in many school districts *despite* state statutes that limit organizing and collective bargaining.

Not surprisingly, the collective-bargaining process has taken on the adversarial nature of the relationship between labor and management. The assumptions that the parties have only divergent, if not opposing, interests and that the satisfaction of any party's interests represents a loss to the other party have rarely been questioned over the years. As a result, collective

bargaining in many districts has become an unbearably contentious process.

The very shape of the agreements that emerge from this contentious process is affected by the characteristics of the process itself. Emerging from long hours of late-night negotiations against punitive deadlines come large volumes of detailed rules delineating the use of authority and discretion, pages of salary schedules, and lists of contingencies for every possible exception. If a collective-bargaining agreement is a set of solutions to some set of perceived problems, the analysis of most agreements would demonstrate that the problem being addressed by the agreements is the relationship between the adults in the district.

The demands of systematic education reform have caused labor and management to consider whether they have some mutual interests and whether adversarial collective bargaining is the best way to achieve agreements to solve the problem of low student achievement. Similarly, as the parties address the varied needs of students, parents, and communities, they are finding that fixed contract terms and centralized policies for all conditions in a school district may hamper responsiveness and innovation.

The innovations in this chapter are illustrations of the ways in which both the process of collective bargaining and the forms of collective agreements are changing to support education reform.

INTEREST-BASED BARGAINING

Interest-based bargaining (IBB) is a departure from "positional bargaining" and the traditional, adversarial, industrial model of collective bargaining[1] that assumes bargaining is a zero-sum activity focused on dividing existing resources. In contrast, IBB focuses on parties' *interests* rather than their proposed *positions*, making it possible to explore the values and purposes and to learn whether these interests are shared or complementary.[2] IBB allows parties to identify multiple ways to satisfy interests and to solve problems creatively.

USEFULNESS TO IMPROVING STUDENT ACHIEVEMENT

IBB provides an opportunity to directly address student achievement in the collective-bargaining process. IBB can minimize ritualized adversarial behavior and enable productive relationships to develop, better situating the parties to improve student achievement.

Interest-based bargaining involves a good-faith effort by both sides to understand the other side's needs, interests, and concerns.[3] IBB provides a framework that loosens the rigidity of "positional bargaining" where each party comes to the table with a set of desired terms that it believes is the only way to satisfy its own interests. IBB requires that the parties look beyond specific demands and, through substantive discussion, brainstorm possible solutions. The parties negotiate with one another, instead of against one another. They consider problems to be matters of shared concern, where each has an interest in finding a solution satisfactory to both parties. Successful implementation of IBB does not call upon the parties to compromise principles or neglect the legitimate roles and needs they each have in the employer-employee relationship.

Nancy Peace, noted mediator and facilitator of IBB in public education, believes that a key IBB strategy is in the manner that proposals, or issues, are presented at the outset of the bargaining process. Ordinarily, in traditional bargaining, each party states a problem and identifies a unilaterally determined solution. Both are overstated: the problem is portrayed as worse than it really is and the solution involves a request for more than is expected. A familiar adversarial process is kicked off. Both parties struggle to justify their positions and argue that they are unable or unwilling to meet the demands of the other. They often accuse each other of being unreasonable. There is little probing discussion of the interests that underlie the positions. In contrast, using the IBB approach, the parties initially generate a list of issues, but stop short of proposing one-sided solutions. In IBB, the issues are considered problems, and the negotiations become problem-solving exercises, in which both parties thoughtfully engage. Honest discussion and debate almost preclude posturing and force parties to articulate their actions and reactions effectively.

Some practitioners report that at the outset IBB is process-intense and time consuming, especially if the parties are distrustful of each other. Since successful IBB requires disclosures about interests that make parties feel vulnerable to exploitation, the parties need trust that it is safe to make these disclosures. Trust is built slowly over time and only with mutually satisfying transactions. Ultimately, as the process matures, IBB should save time in collective bargaining by eliminating the rituals of traditional adversarial posturing.

In addition to problem-solving contracts, IBB can lead to several additional benefits. Relationships and trust between the parties can develop that are helpful during implementation of the contract. Implementation problems are fewer and solved at lower and less costly levels of the process. In addition, Peace makes the important point that IBB sometimes goes a long way toward improving the school district's image in a community. This can only be beneficial to the system as a whole since parents and taxpayers do not respond well to districts fractured by labor disputes, no matter who (if anyone) is perceived as being "right."

IBB may be enhanced by the use of a third-party-neutral to facilitate the bargaining process. The facilitator should be someone acceptable to both parties and skilled in helping the parties to identify interests and brainstorm solutions. The facilitator must help the parties sustain a commitment to the IBB process to avoid a breakdown into traditional adversarial bargaining. Most certainly, the parties will require training in the principles and practices of IBB at least the first time it is used but most probably each time to refresh skill sets, bring new players into the process and improve the listening skills and problem-solving capacity of the parties. Even with good intentions, without training, the process can be derailed.[4]

IBB has been successfully used in many types of complex, multi-party interactions, not just collective bargaining. The Consortium for Policy Research in Education (CPRE) reports that IBB has been helpful in negotiating the *principles* of knowledge- and skills-based compensation schedules for teachers, leaving the details of the system to be hammered out by a formal working committee.[5] However, some practitioners in public education find IBB less helpful when the only issue on the table involves money, a topic that easily becomes zero-sum. Precisely because improving student achievement is not a zero-sum concern, IBB is well suited as a process by which innovative collective bargaining terms may be designed.

CASE EXAMPLE:

When Two Sides Move Beyond "Art of Adversarial Bargaining"

BOSTON. Ed Doherty, past president of the Boston Teachers Union (BTU), and then-Superintendent Laval Wilson jointly wrote a thoughtful article describing their experience with IBB — one of the earliest and most complex examples of how IBB helped to achieve a contract focused on education reform.[6] Referring to themselves as "traditional adversaries" who "had long practiced the art of adversarial bargaining," the parties were brought together by interested community power brokers, who threatened to withhold corporate contributions if the union and administration did not agree how to establish site-based shared management of schools during the 1988 collective-bargaining cycle.

From surveys of the BTU membership, Doherty learned that teachers were interested in greater participation in school-level decision-making and professional development. Wilson had experimented with decentralized management in other districts and was in favor of trying it in Boston. Despite agreement on the larger principle of decentralization, the first two months of active negotiations resulted in a face-off between the parties, each advocating their own designs for the new management structure.

Union and administration leaders only began to make progress when the corporate community intervened and asked both sides to use an outside facilitator. Doherty and Wilson attribute the path-breaking contract they achieved to the use of IBB, particularly to a process known as the "option-seeking exercise," during which each party offers options that would satisfy the other party's interests, while "still protecting the interests of his or her own side. Nobody 'owns' any option offered."[7] The parties examine the list of options and then mutually agree to the most satisfactory of the alternatives.

The innovations designed through this contract were not limited to the terms of the agreement. Next, the parties worked together on a joint labor-management steering committee to implement the new school site-based-management structure and on additional projects as they emerged. The authors attribute this to the IBB process:

"Both parties recognize that this contract could not have been achieved through traditional bargaining. ... Through third-party facilitation, the negotiations highlighted the interests of both sides and allowed each side to explore the goals of the other.

The open dialogue at the negotiating table brought to light new alternatives to achieve mutual goals...The process encouraged the development of collaborative options, ways of accommodating both sides' goals and interests.

Despite a profound state fiscal crisis, the powerful education reforms in the contract enabled the parties to return time and time again to key business, municipal and state leaders to garner support for the contract's funding."[8]

CASE EXAMPLE:

N.J. Officials Say Focus Is On Issues, Rather Than 'Win'

PERTH AMBOY, N.J. In 1999, only 34 percent of the 10,000 students in this blue-collar urban school district earned "proficient" ratings in language arts on the New Jersey assessment test. At the same time, a new superintendent introduced interest-based bargaining to the adversarial relationship with the teachers' union, using this innovative approach to achieve a collective-bargaining agreement. This contract established the joint labor-management *Partnership for Academic Excellence* that, among other things, provided district financing for research-based innovations in classroom practice by teachers. The *Partnership* was directed by the Professional Review Committee—a 22-member, multi-stakeholder group that met biweekly to plan strategies to improve professional and student performance. As with the interest-based bargaining sessions, attorneys representing the school board and teachers' union jointly facilitated the Review Committee.

The parties report that interest-based bargaining contributed to shorter, more productive negotiations.[9] Interest-based bargaining helped parties to focus more quickly on their common interest in student achievement. In reflecting on the experience, Director of Labor Relations William Stratton says: "The focus on 'issues,' not 'who' is going to 'win,' puts a whole new spin on the process. It calms the emotions and seeks solutions to the real issues facing education today."[10] Student achievement in the district improved as well. By 2002, 77.7 percent of students achieved "proficient" ratings, doubling the percentage similarly rated just three years earlier.

ADDITIONAL DISTRICTS THAT HAVE USED INTEREST-BASED BARGAINING

- Cincinnati

- Greece, N.Y.

- Groton-Dunstable, Mass.

- Hamilton-Wenham, Mass.

- North Andover, Mass.

- Sudbury, Mass.

- Williamstown, Mass.

ADDITIONAL READING

- Consortium for Policy Research in Education (2001). *Enhancing teacher quality through knowledge and skills based pay.* Philadelphia. Policy Brief RB34.

- Peace, N. (1994). A new way to negotiate: Collaborative bargaining in teacher contract negotiations: The experience in five Massachusetts school districts. *Journal of Law & Education* 24(3):365-387.

- Lum, G. (1996). Collective bargaining in education: Getting started in interest based negotiation. *Journal of the North American Association of Educational Negotiators.* Obtainable from ThoughtBridge. (Glum@Thoughtbridge.com)

CHAPTER FOOTNOTES

1. Susan Moore Johnson and Susan M. Kardos use the term "industrial model of unionism" to refer to the traditional form adopted from heavy manufacturing, which assumes: interests of the parties are in conflict; standard practice is desirable; similarly skilled workers are interchangeable and should be treated alike. See Johnson, S.M. and Kardos, S.M. (2000). Reform bargaining and its promise for school improvement. In Tom Loveless, (Ed) *Conflicting missions? Teachers unions and educational reform.* Washington, D.C.: Brookings Institution.

2. For a full exposition of IBB see: Fisher, R. and Ury, W. (1992). *Getting to yes: Negotiating agreement without giving in.* New York: Houghton Mifflin Co..

3. Nancy Peace is an arbitrator, mediator, and trainer in private practice in Newburyport, Mass. She has assisted school districts throughout Massachusetts in implementing IBB in contract negotiations. Her articles include: Peace, N. (1994). A new way to negotiate: Collaborative bargaining in teacher contract negotiations: The experience in five Massachusetts school districts. *Journal of Law & Education* 24(3):365-387.

4. William Stratton, Director of Human Resources, Perth Amboy, N.J., Public Schools. Personal interview. Nov. 29, 2004.

5. Consortium for Policy Research in Education (CPRE). "Enhancing Teacher Quality through Knowledge and Skills-Based Pay," Page 6.

6. Doherty, E.J. and Wilson, L.S. (1990). The making of a contract for education reform. *Phi Delta Kappan* (6) 791-796. The authors labeled their IBB process: "principled negotiations."

7. Ibid. Page 793.

8. Ibid. Page 796. Ultimately, it did take strike threats and political action to win final support for the contract, but the authors believe these would not have been successful if not for the educational reform the contract promised.

9. Beach, A. and Kaboolian, L. (2003). *Public Service, Public Savings.* Washington, D.C. www.Pslmc.org./pslmc.asp

10. William Stratton, personal correspondence. Dec. 1, 2004.

RESOURCES AND REFERENCES

- **Nancy Peace**
  Mediator & Author
  29 Green Street
  P.O. Box 378
  Newburyport, MA 01950
  Tel: 978.462.3266   Fax: 978.462.3352
  npeace@igc.org

- **Indiana Education Employment Relations Board**
  Indiana Government Center North
  100 N. Senate Avenue, Suite N1049
  Indianapolis, IN 46204-2211
  Tel: 317.233.6620   Fax: 317.233.6632
  www.in.gov/ieerb/training/

- **ThoughtBridge Consulting Group**
  Katrina Robertson Reed
  Consultant, Former Director,
  Human Resources Minneapolis School District
  ThoughtBridge Consulting Group
  3 Bow Street, Cambridge, MA 02138
  Tel: 617.868.8641   Fax: 617.868.8642
  www.thoughtbridge.net
  Robreedk@aol.com

- **Programs for Employment & Workplace Systems (PEWS)**
  Cornell University Programs
  Sally Klingel Sr., Extension Associate
  146 Ives Hall Garden Avenue Cornell University
  Ithaca, NY 14853-3901
  Tel: 607.255.7022   Fax: 607.255.0574
  www.ilr.cornell.edu/extension/pews/c_home.html
  slk12@cornell.edu

- **Perth Amboy Federation of Teachers**
  Donna Chiera, President
  Norman Tankiewicz, District Representative
  1429 Kearny Avenue, Perth Amboy, NJ 08861
  Tel: 732.442.7788
  www.paf-aft.org/indexbak.html
  pafaft@aol.com

- **Perth Amboy Public Schools**
  William Stratton, Director of Human Resources
  Vivian Rodriguez, Assistant Superintendent
  for Learning & Educational Services
  178 Barracks Street, Perth Amboy, NJ 08661
  Tel: 732.376.6200   Fax: 732.826.2644
  www.paps.net

SALARY BENCHMARKING

'Salary benchmarking' is the practice of determining
teacher salaries in the collective-bargaining process
by referring to indicators outside the district.
Salary scales of nearby school districts set the standard,
rather than traditional formulas such as "cost of living
increases." Parties negotiate the list of referent districts
and the formula that will determine the relationship
between the district's new salary scale and the scale
at referent districts.

USEFULNESS
TO IMPROVING
STUDENT
ACHIEVEMENT

The primary benefit of benchmarking is that it helps districts be more competitive in recruiting, hiring, and retaining successful, highly qualified teachers. Secondarily, it saves time and reduces conflict on money matters, enabling parties to spend more time and energy for collaboration and negotiation on strategies for improving student achievement.

Salary benchmarking is premised on two theories:

- Teacher quality affects student achievement; and
- There is a competitive labor market for high-quality teachers, operating on differentials in salary and working conditions.

Eric Hanushek, an education economist, tested the first theory and found that, "The estimated difference in annual growth between having a good and having a bad teacher can be more than one grade-level equivalent in test performance."[11] In later work, Hanushek and others found that teacher quality is the most important determinant of school quality.[12]

If the market is competitive, evidence suggests that salary and working conditions do affect the ability of a district to attract and retain high-quality teachers.[13] Benchmarking bases the salary formula on a negotiated set of mutually accepted goals and standards, addressing conditions as well as future needs. Benchmarking may incorporate long-term goals, financially unachievable in the short run, but accepted by both parties as a priority where 'catch-up' is needed in order to attract and retain high-quality teachers.

Salary benchmarking can benefit all parties to contract negotiations. The practice makes the disparities with competitor districts more visible to all of the school district stakeholders, not just the union and administration. As a result of the comparison, salaries can be defined by a strategy to improve student achievement rather than by power or bargaining history.

Practitioners believe that it is easier to agree to the list of districts with which comparisons must be made and the formula for benchmarking than to negotiate a detailed salary schedule. Once established, a formula may not have to be adjusted from one bargaining cycle to another, although both parties will want to preserve the right to do so.

Benchmarking enables parties to concentrate more on substantive reform because they:

- Save substantial amounts of time, otherwise spent on protracted salary negotiations
- Minimize the direct cost of hiring professional negotiators
- Reduce indirect costs of district staff time needed to support professional negotiators by supplying them with numbers, comparisons, budgets, projections, etc., and
- Preserve emotional energy and labor-management relationships

While not every district can be "above average" in its compensation structure, it is still possible to use benchmarking. Salary benchmarking does not require that the parties agree to match or exceed pay levels in other districts but to peg compensation relative to identified districts. Relevant factors that distinguish a district, such as tax base or the value of benefit packages can be factored into the benchmarking process. When done carefully, salary benchmarking has produced satisfactory and fair results.

CASE EXAMPLE:

Rochester, N.Y., Sees Benchmarking As Way To Retain Experienced Teachers

ROCHESTER, N.Y. The City School District of Rochester and the Rochester Teachers Association agreed in 2000 to benchmark teachers' salaries in response to a survey of teachers who had left the district with between five to eight years of experience. As part of an effort to retain experienced teachers, the parties began to look at more competitive contracts.[14]

Their July 2002 collective-bargaining agreement states six basic steps and principles in their process:

- The parties identify a comparison group—school districts paying salaries within the top third of the county region. The parties state their intention to remain "reasonably competitive" with the comparison group at designated career junctures for teachers (e.g., entry level, five years' experience, 10 years' experience, etc.). They specify that their formula for salary increases shall "provide the basis for design of a formula intended to inform bargaining for specific increases in salaries for unit members."[15]
- The parties agree that they will determine the most recent average salary increases in the comparative districts, and then "apply the result in an agreed-upon manner so as to achieve reasonably competitive salaries for unit members, particularly at the designated career junctures."
- The parties express their present intention that the formula will survive the duration of the current contract, though in the next section they state their understanding that they are not contractually bound beyond the current contract.
- The parties clarify that either party may reject the formula as a basis for determining salaries upon expiration of the current contract, and a

timeline related to the state budget cycle is specified.

- The parties state that if the current formula is rejected for the next contract, and another formula or process for establishing pay rates has not been agreed upon by a specified date, teachers will all advance one step on the existing salary scale until settlement is reached.

- Step advancements that occur because the formula has been rejected and not replaced shall be retroactive to the first day following expiration of the current contract.

The current superintendent and union president in Rochester both cite the salary benchmarking process in Rochester as a significant step forward. They suggest that there may be other contract areas in which benchmarking could reduce the strain and tedium of collective bargaining, enabling parties to focus instead on creative reforms that promote student success.[16]

ADDITIONAL DISTRICTS THAT HAVE
USED SALARY BENCHMARKING

- Andover, Mass.
- Webster Central School District, N.Y.

RESOURCES AND REFERENCES

- **Rochester Public Schools**
  CONTACT: Manuel J. Rivera, Superintendent
  131 West Broad Street, Rochester, NY 14614
  Tel: 585.262 8100
  www.rcsdk12.org
  manuel.rivera@rcsdk12.org

- **Rochester Teachers Association**
  CONTACT: Adam Urbanski, President
  30 N. Union Street, Suite 301, Rochester, NY 14607
  Tel: 585.546.2681
  www.rochesterteachers.com
  urbanski@rochesterteachers.com

CHAPTER FOOTNOTES

11. Hanushek, E.A. (1992) The trade-off between child quantity and quality. In *Journal of Political Economy* 100(1):84-117.

12. Rivkin, S.G., Hanushek, E.A. and Kain, J.F. (1998). *Teachers, schools and academic achievement.* Paper presented at Association of Public Policy Analysis and Management, New York, N.Y.

13. See Murnane, R.J., Singer, J.D., Willett, J. B., Kemple, J.J. and Olson, R.J. (1991). *Who will teach? Policies that matter.* Cambridge, Mass.: Harvard University Press. Also see Odden, A. and Kelley, C. 1997. *Paying Teachers for What They know and do: New and smarter compensation strategies to improve schools.* Thousand Oaks, Calif.: Corwin Press.

14. Correspondence with former superintendent Clifford B. Janey, February 2004.

15. Agreement Between the City School District of Rochester, N.Y., and the Rochester Teachers Association. July 1, 2002. Section 46, 3a(1&2).

16. Panel discussion with Adam Urbanski, chief negotiator and president of the Rochester Teachers Association, and Manuel Rivera, superintendent, at event sponsored by Worcester Regional Research Bureau and the Rennie Center for Education Research & Policy at MassINC, Worcester, Mass., Dec. 1, 2003.

CONTRACT WAIVERS & OVERRIDES

Increasingly, contracts include waivers or override language that allow the parties to sidestep specific contractual language in limited circumstances and for specific purposes, usually related to reform efforts. Waivers and overrides frequently have temporary effect only, and are always subject to joint approval.

USEFULNESS TO IMPROVING STUDENT ACHIEVEMENT

As specific changes are needed in the learning environment to address student achievement, the terms of the collective-bargaining agreement can be modified to accommodate those changes.

While contract waivers and overrides may seem familiar and have been part of collective bargaining in most settings, education reform has extended the scope and frequency of their use. Many contracts now anticipate the need for substantial changes to accommodate the innovation of reform efforts and provide defined mechanisms to make changes during the life of multi-year contracts. Institutionalized in contract language, waiver provisions further legitimize concern for student achievement, making it clear that "business as usual" should not continue if students are not learning. They normalize the change process through defined procedures and standing committees to consider needed changes. They assign joint responsibility for improvements to both parties.

In most cases, all parties at the local level must ratify the changes proposed under these provisions. In some circumstances, parents' representatives may be involved in decision-making. While the thresholds for ratification might appear high, it is also the case that necessary changes are more likely to be implemented and affect performance if the vast majority of teachers agree to them.

CASE EXAMPLE:

Worcester, Mass., Uses Side Letter To Try Small Learning Communities

WORCESTER, MASS. The Worcester School District, with the support of the Carnegie Foundation for the Advancement of Teaching, has been working on the creation of small learning communities at the secondary level in an effort to improve student outcomes. In the process, the Worcester School Committee and the Educational Association of Worcester (EAW) recognized that their plans for effective small learning communities might require substantive changes to the existing district-wide collective-bargaining agreement, as well as a collaborative problem-solving process that will be less cumbersome than collective bargaining. Accordingly, in 2003 the Worcester School Committee and the EAW entered into a side letter, "to accomplish the flexibilities required to make the small learning communities successful without making permanent modifications to the underlying collective bargaining agreement."[18]

The side letter is of limited duration, expiring at the end of the 2004-2005 school year. It is also limited in scope, prohibiting changes to grievance procedures, supervision and evaluation, transfers, reductions in force, and teacher dismissal. The parties clarified their intent, stating explicitly in the side letter that this waiver was not intended to affect governance issues, but rather to allow flexibility in operational areas, including meetings, workday, scheduling, hours and work load, block scheduling, duties, preparation time, and "such other areas not specifically excluded herein."[19]

The side letter requires that contract waiver proposals be carefully scrutinized. Plans for small learning communities must be written, and all areas of the master agreement that might be affected by the plan must be specifically identified. The plan must also state the proposed manner of dealing with those sections of the contract. The committee and the

EXAMPLES OF CONTRACT & SIDE LETTER LANGUAGE

Side Letter, Small Learning Communities. Executed Feb. 26, 2003 by the Worcester School Committee and the Educational Association of Worcester.

It is agreed by the parties that the formal plans, as drafted, and as implemented in certain cases, involve changes to the terms and conditions of employment of the teaches and assistant principals at the secondary schools which would require decisional bargaining…the Parties will agree to utilize this Side Letter and the agreements contained herein to accomplish the flexibilities required to make the small learning communities successful without making permanent modifications to the underlying collective bargaining agreement. The parties are in agreement that this Side Letter shall not authorize modifications in the following areas of the contract: Grievance Procedure; Leaves of Absence with or without pay; Sick Leave; Supervision and Evaluation; Transfers; Reduction In Force; and Dismissal of Teachers…[17]

executive board of the association must approve the full plan. If they do, two-thirds of the teachers in the proposed small learning community must vote by secret ballot to accept the plan before it can be implemented.

CASE EXAMPLE:

Florida District Creates Panel To Review Waiver Requests

DUVAL COUNTY, FLA. The 2002-2005 Duval County teachers' contract creates a joint Contract Waiver and Oversight Committee "…authorized to provide oversight for contract compliance and to review contract waiver requests necessitated by new innovative programs and/or school improvement efforts."[20] The eight-member committee includes the

**2002-2005 Agreement between
the Duval County Teachers Union
and the Duval County School District**

A committee comprised of the President of DTU and three designees, the General Director, Human Resource Services, and three designees of the Superintendent, shall function as the Contract Waiver and Oversight Committee. The Contract Oversight and Waiver Committee will be authorized to provide oversight for contract compliance and to review contract waiver requests necessitated by new innovative programs and/or school improvement efforts…

**2003-2006 Agreement Between
United Teachers of New Orleans
and Orleans Parish School Board. Article 53.**

The BOARD and the UNION recognize the need of the District to take meaningful steps to increase the academic performance of students. The implementation of programs and initiatives directed at increasing student achievement levels requires the BOARD and the UNION to be flexible in applying policies, rules and regulations of the District and provisions of the UTNO/OPSB Collective Bargaining Agreement. On occasions, this flexibility necessitates the waiving of provisions of the Teacher Collective Bargaining Agreement. To this end, the BOARD and the UNION have agreed to the following procedures for granting waivers from complying with provisions of the OPSB/UTNO Teacher Collective Bargaining Agreement.

**July 1, 2002, Agreement between
City School District of Rochester
and the Rochester Teachers Association Rochester…..**

[Lead teachers shall] agree to accept assignments which meet school needs regardless of contractual/seniority rights….

union president and three union designees, as well as the human resources director and three designees appointed by the superintendent.

As in Worcester, there is a fairly elaborate review and approval process that must be completed before contract waivers can take effect. Written waiver requests must be reviewed and approved by the regional superintendent involved, as well as by the Contract Waiver and Oversight Committee. Submissions to the committee must include supporting documentation. The committee may request personal appearances by teachers and/or members of the administration to discuss the waiver proposal. If the committee approves a waiver request, it issues a recommendation to the executive board of the union and the superintendent's task force on waivers, both of which must agree before a waiver can be granted. Significantly, waivers can be approved for periods of no longer than the remainder of the school year. After that, the collective-bargaining teams for the respective parties determine whether they will be continued.[21]

CASE EXAMPLE:

New Orleans Board, Union Negotiate Collective-Bargaining Waiver

NEW ORLEANS. The board and the union in New Orleans jointly recognize the value of contract flexibility in efforts to improve academic performance through innovation. Accordingly, they have negotiated an article entitled "Collective Bargaining Provision Waiver," describing a process whereby 70 percent of the members of the bargaining unit at a particular school may agree by secret ballot to seek a contract waiver. The union's executive board and the board of education must both approve a waiver request.[22]

CASE EXAMPLE:

Rochester Officials Agree on Flexibility To Place Teachers in Struggling Schools

ROCHESTER, N.Y. The City School District of Rochester and the Rochester Teachers Association have negotiated a provision that allows seniority provisions to be overridden during teacher assignment, in order to improve the performance of struggling schools. Among other provisions, the contract defines "Lead Teachers" as highly qualified teachers with additional responsibilities that are intended to shape and improve public education in Rochester (as measured by student attainment and performance).[23] To facilitate the strategic placement of teachers, the contract contains an override clause, stating that Lead Teachers shall agree to accept assignments that meet school needs *regardless of*

contractual/seniority rights.[24] This enables schools to pursue strategies such as placing Lead Teachers in difficult teaching assignments, where their advanced knowledge and skills can have the most impact on student outcomes.

OTHER DISTRICTS THAT HAVE
USED CONTRACT WAIVERS & OVERRIDES

- Cleveland
- Palm Beach County, Fla.
- Pittsburgh
- Seattle [25]

CHAPTER FOOTNOTES

17. *Side Letter, Small Learning Communities.* Executed Feb. 26, 2003, by the Worcester School Committee and the Educational Association of Worcester.

18. See Worcester Regional *Research Bureau (2003). Education reform and collective bargaining: C for compatibility.* Worcester, Mass. Report No. 03-05.

19. 2002-2005 Agreement between the Duval County Teachers Union and the Duval County School District, Article IV, Sec.2B.

20. Ibid.

21. 2003-2006 Agreement between United Teachers of New Orleans and Orleans Parish School Board. Article 53.

22. July 1, 2002, Agreement between City School District of Rochester and the Rochester Teachers Association, Sec. 52-11.

23. Ibid, Sec. 12-f-1.

24. In Seattle, the contract states that the terms of the Staff Training, Assistance and Review Program (STAR) will supersede the terms of the collective-bargaining agreement if there is a conflict between the two documents. Memorandum of Understanding Concerning The STAR Program Between the Seattle School Committee and the Seattle Education Association. Section A-6.

25. The Teachers Urban Reform Network (TURN) founded in 1995 is a group of teachers' union locals belonging to the American Federation of Teachers (AFT) or the National Education Association (NEA). TURN describes itself as a union-led effort to restructure the nation's teachers' unions to promote education reform. The following districts are members: Albuquerque, N.Mex.; Bellevue, Wash.; Boston; Cincinnati; Columbus, Ohio; Dade Country, Fla.; Denver; Hammond, Ind.; Los Angeles; Memphis, Tenn.; Minneapolis; Montgomery County, Md.; New York; Pinellas County, Fla.; Pittsburgh; Rochester, N.Y.; San Diego; San Francisco; Seattle; Toledo, Ohio; Westerly, R.I. See www.turnexchange.net

RESOURCES AND REFERENCES

- **Duval County Public Schools**
  Vicki Reynolds, Assistant Superintendent
  Human Resource Services Dept.
  1701 Prudential Drive, Jacksonville, FL 32207-8182
  Tel: 904.390.2936
  www.educationcentral.org

- **Duval County Teachers Union**
  Terri Brady, President
  1601 Atlantic Boulevard, Jacksonville, FL 32207
  Tel: 904.396.4063   Fax: 904.396.9389
  www.dtujax.com
  dtujax@aol.com

- **New Orleans Public Schools***
  Anthony Amato, Superintendent
  3510 General de Gaulle Drive, New Orleans, LA 70114
  Tel: 504.304.5702
  www.nops.k12.la.us

- **United Teachers of New Orleans***
  Brenda Mitchell, President
  4650 Paris Avenue Suite 209, New Orleans, LA 70122
  Tel: 504.282.1026   Fax: 504.283.S057
  www.utno.org

- **Rochester Public Schools**
  Manuel J. Rivera, Superintendent
  131 West Broad Street, Rochester, NY 14614
  Tel: 585.262 8100
  www.rcsdk12.org
  manuel.rivera@rcsdk12.org

- **Rochester Teachers Association**
  Adam Urbanski, President
  30 N. Union Street, Suite 301, Rochester, NY 14607
  Tel: 585.546.2681
  www.rochesterteachers.com
  urbanski@rochesterteachers.com

- **Worcester Public Schools**
  James Caradonio, Superintendent
  20 Irving Street , Worcester, MA 01609
  Tel: 508.799.3115   Fax: 508.799.3119
  www.wpsweb.com
  caradonio@worc.k12.ma.us

- **Educational Association of Worcester**
  Cheryl DelSignore, President
  397 Grove Street, Worcester, MA 01605
  Tel: 508.791.3296   Fax: 508.754.2461
  Worcester.massteacher.org
  cheryl.eaw@gmail.com

* Note: New Orleans contact information was gathered prior to Hurricane Katrina. It may no longer be accurate.

THIN CONTRACTS

In comparison to traditional encyclopedic contracts, "thin" contracts are abbreviated agreements negotiated at the district level to address basic issues and standardize conditions across the district. Thin contracts address issues such as base compensation, benefits, and compliance with legislative mandates. Supplemental, more detailed contracts are negotiated at the school site level to address local needs, concerns, and working conditions. Thin contracts and local supplements recognize that important differences and needs exist among schools within a district. They shift more control over policy and programming to the local level, requiring that teachers and administrators at the school site negotiate comprehensive agreements about the day-to-day operations.

USEFULNESS TO IMPROVING STUDENT ACHIEVEMENT

With thin contracts, decisions affecting teaching and learning are made closer to the school site and can be tailored to meet the specific needs of students, practitioners, and the community. The two-level contract allows for flexibility within a district and avoids the rigidity of one-size-fits-all conditions.

The concept of a "thin contract" goes hand in hand with other reform efforts that are focused on breaking out of the "one-size-fits-all" bargaining model to focus attention on local needs and conditions for improving student achievement. Sandra Feldman, former president of the American Federation of Teachers, was one of the first and, perhaps, biggest proponents of thin contracts. The Teacher Union Reform Network (TURN)[26] has also proposed thin contracts as a model for shifting detailed collective bargaining away from district-level negotiations and to school settings where terms can be more sensitive and responsive to local needs.

An important distinction between the thin contract model and other reforms is that the thin contract model does not contemplate local agreements as *exceptions* to a master agreement. Under the thin contract model, school site agreements are the norm. Thin contract supplements do not have to be authorized by contract waivers, contract over-ride clauses, or a special contractual recognition of a specific site (such as a small learning community, pilot, or charter school). Thin contract supplements serve as the only place that local school issues—student performance targets, resource allocation, class size, professional development programs, and similar matters—are contractually addressed.

One concern with the thin contract model is that site-level leaders—school principals and union building representatives—assume more of the burden for collective bargaining, despite being already overburdened with the instructional and management demands of education reform. In reality, thin contracts can be achieved at lower costs than assumed, especially when professional negotiators from the district level assist with local level discussions. While site-level bargaining may require a greater investment of time and resources by schools, the ensuing benefits of this "hands-on" involvement over traditional district-level collective bargaining are significant over time. Traditional collective bargaining typically results in generalized work rules that lead to local school inefficiencies and time-consuming problems for principals and union representatives. Conversely, when parties have an opportunity to present and negotiate rules that best match their school's conditions, the resulting work rules better fit the school's needs and the specific desires of the school's teachers than a district-level agreement.

CASE EXAMPLE:

N.Y. Charter School Finds Flexibility In Nine-Page Contract Agreement

AMBER CHARTER SCHOOL - NEW YORK. In contrast to the very extensive 2000-2003 agreement between the New York City Board of Education and the UFT, the 2002-2004 agreement between the UFT and Amber Charter School is a "thin contact,"

CONTRACT LANGUAGE EXAMPLE: THIN CONTRACTS

2002-2004 Agreement between The United Federation of Teachers and The Amber Charter School.

Introduction
   WHEREAS, the parties desire to maintain a collaborative relationship beyond their collective bargaining relationship so as to provide the best opportunity for Amber Charter School to succeed in its educational mission;

   NOW THEREFORE, the parties have entered into this unique Agreement in the expectation that the flexibility it provides will help Amber School grow and thrive, to the benefit of the entire Amber School family.

   Article 2, Personnel Manual
   The Amber Charter School Personnel Policy and Procedures Employee Manual ("Manual") describes the general conditions and benefits applicable to Amber School employees. Bargaining Unit Members are covered by the Manual, and it is incorporated into this Agreement, to the extent its terms are not contrary to or inconsistent with this Agreement.

which is nine pages long, including a one-page payroll deduction form. The agreement contains 13 articles addressing almost exclusively matters of compensation, benefits, and employment security.[27]

The preamble of the agreement states the parties' desire:

- "...to maintain a collaborative relationship beyond their collective bargaining relationship so as to provide the best opportunity for Amber Charter School to succeed in its educational mission."
- The preamble also states the parties' expectation that the flexibility provided by their 'unique agreement' will help Amber Charter School grow and thrive, to the benefit of the entire "Amber School Family."[28] Two additional clauses in the Amber contract are particularly important to understanding thin contracts.

Article Two specifically incorporates the school's pre-existing Personnel Policy and Procedures Employee Manual, making it part of the master agreement (to the extent that the manual's terms are not contrary to or inconsistent with the UFT-Amber agreement). Amber's previously adopted personnel policy manual serves as the local supplement to a thin master contract. This model is helpful because it demonstrates how a local supplement can function as a personnel handbook might—covering operational teaching and learning issues, having contractual status, and describing the rights and responsibilities of teachers and school administrations within each building or small school site.

The second clause shifts policy work to the local faculty of this small school. The clause addresses continuing salary discussions and states that the parties have agreed to involve the Amber School teachers in considering alternative and/or supplemental compensation systems. The agreement further states that the parties wish to encourage the Amber School faculty to use their special skills,

achievements, talents, and qualifications to design and implement projects that will enhance the Amber School experience.

RESOURCES AND REFERENCES

- **Teacher Union Reform Network (TURN)**
  Adam Urbanski, Director
  Rochester Teachers Association
  30 N. Union St., Suite 301, Rochester, NY 14607-1345
  Tel: 585.546.2681
  www.rochesterteachers.com
  urbanski@rochesterteachers.com

- **United Federation of Teachers (UFT)**
  Randi Weingarten, President
  Lucille Swaim, Coordinator of Negotiations
  52 Broadway Avenue, New York, NY 10004
  Tel: 212.777.7500
  www.uft.org

- **Amber Charter School Personnel Policy and Procedures Employee Manual**, 11.24.03

- **Amber Charter School**
  220 East 106th Street, New York, NY 10029
  Tel: 212.534.9667   Fax: 212.534.6225
  http://ambercharter.echalk.com

CHAPTER FOOTNOTES

26. Article headings are: Recognition, Personnel Manual, Due Process, Rates of Pay, Maintenance of Benefits, Union Security, Payroll Deduction of Union Dues, Layoff and Recall, No Strike-No Lockout, Conformity to Law, Amendment, Duration, and Termination.

27. 2002-2004 Agreement between the United Federation of Teachers and the Amber Charter School. Page 1.

28. Nov. 24, 2003, telephone interview with Rita Siegel, labor relations officer and attorney for Albuquerque School District.

LIVING CONTRACTS

Living contracts remain open to modification during the course of their stated term, adapting to evolving circumstances unforeseen at the time they are drafted. The parties define an ongoing collaborative process to identify and design changes to existing language as need arises. Addressing the problem of multi-year contracts with terms no longer appropriate to the dynamic, innovative demands of education reform, living contracts allow for flexibility and innovation.

USEFULNESS TO IMPROVING STUDENT ACHIEVEMENT

As parties seek to improve student outcomes with new strategies or programs, existing prescriptive contract language and re-opening the contract are not insurmountable barriers to reform.

"Living contracts" are comprehensive, district-wide collective-bargaining contracts that contain provisions to allow continual renegotiation and modification during the course of their stated term. More radical than waivers or override language, "living contracts" make provisions for continual negotiations and make the assumption that fundamental changes are possible through the work of a standing committee that negotiates new terms. Living contracts allow the parties to operate outside of the boundaries of negotiated contract language, in accordance with a process designed to protect the rights of the parties.

Living contracts remain in full effect unless modified through a joint process involving labor and management representatives and ratification by some stated majority of union members. Members of the negotiating committee meet to discuss issues and concerns of mutual interest as they arise. While living contract committees can be powerful vehicles for promoting reform between negotiations, they are not necessarily focused on reform or student outcomes. They are sometimes used to foresee conflict and head off grievances. Living contracts also may be used to facilitate the next round of negotiations by studying issues outside of the negotiating process.[29]

CASE EXAMPLE:

Rochester Uses 'Living Contract' To Tackle Issues of Mutual Interest

ROCHESTER, N.Y. The current contract in Rochester establishes and charges a Living Contract Committee. This committee is a joint labor-management committee, comprised of at least two and not more than four representatives from both the union and the district. Neither the superintendent nor the union president may serve on the committee; however, their participation in committee meetings is permitted as deemed necessary or appropriate. The district's chief legal counsel must be one of the district's representatives on the committee.[30]

The Living Contract Committee is authorized "to discuss any issue of mutual interest or concern and to reach tentative agreements on issues in a timely manner without delaying action until the expiration *and re-negotiation of the collective bargaining agreement.*" The Living Contract Committee has the power to *amend* the collective-bargaining agreement—*"provided that any substantive amendments shall be subject to internal ratification and approval processes of the district and the union."* [31]

The committee is charged to:

- Meet monthly on a regularly scheduled basis
- Administer and implement the contract and to resolve disputes in its interpretation and application
- Train teachers and district staff concerning contract responsibility and good practice
- Establish *temporary* joint subcommittees to address contract issues
- Revise the provisions of the agreement in order to clarify language and meaning, correct contradictions or inconsistencies, remove outdated language, and organize and streamline it

CONTRACT LANGUAGE EXAMPLE: LIVING CONTRACTS

Toledo, 2001-March 31, 2004. Memorandum of Understanding.

In addition, the parties recognize the need for resolving mutual problems and concerns as they arise. Both parties agree in principle that an ongoing problem-solving process is necessary and each is committed to achieving mutually established goals and objectives to that end.... To formalize the implementation of this memorandum, the wages, hours, terms, and conditions of employment as set forth in this collective bargaining agreement shall continue

The Living Contract Committee is specifically empowered to address teacher transfer issues outside of regularly bargained transfer provisions. The committee may consider and *approve* such transfers. Involuntary transfers cannot be grieved.[32]

CASE EXAMPLE:

Toledo Contract Allows Changes At School Building Level

TOLEDO, OHIO. The 2001-2004 Toledo contract contains a provision allowing contract modification *at the building level.* Each school has a Federation Building Committee, defined as the teacher committee authorized by the union, and elected by the teachers in the building. The Federation Building Committee is entitled to meet with the school principal at least twice per month to address school operations. The normal scope of discussions includes building-level policy formation or modification—consistent with the master contract. "However, if either the principal, or the committee, or both, desire to modify certain to remain in effect and will be changed or modified on an ongoing basis with the mutual consent of the parties. This Memorandum of Understanding will remain in effect throughout the term of the current collective bargaining agreement, i.e. November 30, 2000.

Eugene. 2003-2005 Agreement between the Eugene Education Association and the Eugene School District 4J. Article XVI.

- **16.2 Joint Administration Committee:** The District and Association will establish and jointly participate in a contract administration committee titled Joint Contract Administration Committee, hereinafter JCAC.

- **16.2.1 Purpose:** The purpose of the JCAC will be to review proposals from the District or Association to waive or modify any terms of the agreement.
- **16.2.2 Decision-Making:** The JCAC will make decisions by consensus. If the JCAC is unable to reach agreement, action to modify or waive the agreement will not be taken except as provided by other terms of this agreement.
- **16.2.3 Composition:** The JCAC will be composed of at least two (2) representatives appointed by the District and two (2) representatives appointed by the Association. The JCAC membership composition may be changed as the District and Association deem appropriate.

contractual provisions, such proposed modification shall be reviewed by a joint committee appointed equally by the Superintendent and the Federation President and its mutual decision to modify such contract terms shall constitute consent to modify. Such modifications shall be reduced to writing and forwarded to the school, and shall be applicable at the school and enforceable as a collateral agreement."[33]

CASE EXAMPLE:

Eugene, Ore., Uses 'Interim' Process To Meet Between Contract Talks

EUGENE, ORE. In Eugene, Ore., the district and the union engage in a process they call "interim bargaining." The system allows the parties to meet between contracts to deal with problems and issues as they arise. The parties may bargain new language, or not. If they do, their language can eventually become binding, upon passage of a series of approvals, including that of the Joint

Contract Administration Committee (JCAC). Agreements approved by JCAC take effect once made, but become part of the negotiated collective-bargaining agreement only following incorporation in the next formal contract negotiation.

JCAC is subject to Oregon's open meeting laws, so its actions are non-confidential. The committee meets frequently, and operates on a consensus basis. Its purpose, powers, and composition are stated in the collective-bargaining agreement, but without much detail. According to Association President Paul Duchin, JCAC is much more significant than it would appear from the contract. It meets nearly every two weeks. It assigns small groups to resolve problems, and/or attempt to bargain solutions subject to later approval. While there is often disagreement among members of JCAC, Duchin states that overall it is extremely helpful in creating understanding and respectful relationships among members of the association and the administration.

OTHER DISTRICTS THAT HAVE USED LIVING CONTRACTS

- Albuquerque, N.Mex.
- Minneapolis

RESOURCES AND REFERENCES

- **Eugene Education Association**
  Paul Duchin, President
  2815 Coburg Road, Eugene, OR 97408
  (541) 345-0338

- **Eugene School District 4J**
  George Russell, Superintendent
  200 North Monroe Street, Eugene, OR 97402
  Tel: 541-687-3123   Fax: 541-687-3691
  www.4j.lane.edu
  Russell_g@4j.lane.edu

- **Rochester Public Schools**
  Manuel J. Rivera, Superintendent
  131 West Broad Street, Rochester, NY 14614
  Tel: 585.262 8100
  www.rcsdk12.org
  manuel.rivera@rcsdk12.org

- **Rochester Teachers Association**
  Adam Urbanski, President
  30 N. Union Street, Suite 301, Rochester, NY 14607
  Tel: 585.546.2681
  www.rochesterteachers.com
  urbanski@rochesterteachers.com

- **Toledo Federation of Teachers**
  Francine Lawrence, President
  111 S. Byrne Road, Toledo, OH 43615
  Tel: 419-535-3013   Fax: 419-535-0478
  www.tft250.org

- **Toledo Public Schools**
  Eugene T.W. Sanders, Superintendent
  420 E. Manhattan Blvd. Toledo, OH 43608-1267
  Tel: 419-729-8200
  www.tps.org

CHAPTER FOOTNOTES

29. See generally Section 50, Living Contract Committee, July 1, 2002, contract between the City School District of Rochester and the Rochester Teachers Association.

30. Section 50, Living Contract Committee, July 1, 2002, contract between the City School District of Rochester and the Rochester Teachers Association.

31. Ibid.

32. 2001-2004 Agreement between Toledo Federation of Teachers and the Toledo Public Schools. Article I, Section E-3.

33. See the 1999-03 Chicago Agreement Article 12—Re-engineering Failing Schools.

CONTRACT LANGUAGE ON STUDENT ACHIEVEMENT

Not long ago one could read through hundreds of pages of contract language and never come across the word "student," let alone an explicit concern about student achievement. While there were innumerable regulations outlining expected behavior of the adults in the school system, or limiting their discretion and autonomy, parties often did not articulate the joint purpose of their working relationship as a focus on student achievement. Student needs were often lost in the familiar struggle between labor and management and negotiations that often served predominantly adult interests.

In contrast, some collective-bargaining agreements now explicitly recognize students as the primary client of their working relationship. In these instances, negotiating parties typically attempt to set a new tone for their relationship, moving from a competitive stance to a position that is more collaborative and explicitly focused on improving academic achievement. Similarly, community expectations that teachers and districts will work together to produce good educational results are explicitly acknowledged as legitimate.

USEFULNESS TO IMPROVING STUDENT ACHIEVEMENT

The parties insert language into the contract explicitly stating that the purpose of their relationship is students' welfare, their academic achievement, and the improved performance of the public school district in meeting these goals. In so doing, parties emphasize student needs and articulate their shared interest in improving student achievement.

The school reform and standards movements have changed the focus and content of some collective-bargaining agreements to reflect a joint commitment to students and high performance standards. Some district contracts contain discrete sections on school reform, citing a new urgency in breaking old patterns for the purpose of improving performance.[34] Other districts use side letters or memoranda of understanding to adjust their focus, if they are not yet willing to adapt the contract formally.

Words do not necessarily change actions and attitudes, but this step can make a difference in the world of collective bargaining. When parties use the collective-bargaining agreement to jointly declare that their joint, primary purpose is the creation and maintenance of strong schools to benefit students, the agreement can help to focus teachers and administrators on goals that extend beyond their own immediate contractual advantage. At the very least, parties discussed this language and agreed to insert it. At the other extreme, this language may guide the parties' relationship and implementation

CONTRACT LANGUAGE EXAMPLES: LANGUAGE ON STUDENT ACHIEVEMENT

2001-2003 Agreement Between The Board of Education of Special School District #1 and The Minneapolis Federation of Teachers

Preamble
This agreement is dedicated to doing better.

We exist to ensure that all students learn. We support their growth into knowledgeable, skilled and confident citizens capable of succeeding in their work, personal and family life into the 21st century.

2004-2007 Agreement Between The Providence Teachers Union, AFT Local 958 and The Providence School Board.

Preamble
Whereas, the Providence School Board and the Providence Teachers Union are committed to planning and implementing educational programs of the highest caliber designed to meet the multifaceted needs of our diverse student population, and

Whereas, in the pursuit of this common goal we also share the fundamental beliefs about educational philosophy and the nature of our joint responsibility to establish and maintain collaborative working relationship based on trust, mutual respect, clear and direct communication, and a commitment to shared decision making, and …

Whereas, The School Board and The City of Providence Teachers Union desire to promote good relations among certified teachers and between the School Board and the Union in the best interest of high quality education in the Providence school system…

City and County of Denver, Sept. 1, 2002 – Aug. 31, 2005

Statement of Beliefs
The Board and the Association share the belief that providing a high quality education for the children of Denver is the paramount objective of the District…In negotiating this Agreement, the Board and the Association, with the concurrence of the Community, have three major goals for joint school reform efforts:

- Greater success for all students as reflected in higher achievement.
- A significantly higher completion rate that moves the District toward its goal of graduating all students from the K-12 educational program.
- An improvement in the Community's level of confidence that the Denver Public Schools, as an institution, provides effective education for all students.

of the contract. The inclusion of student-focused contract language also creates a legitimate expectation on the part of other stakeholders that the parties will follow through on their commitment and that there is a standard by which to hold them accountable.

Critics ask if the addition of language has a real impact on the performance of the school district. While a systematic evaluation of the cause and effect relationship has not been performed, it is interesting to note that this language is often found in districts where other innovative practices are found, including innovations in the collective-bargaining agreement. Such research may also provide insight on how best to strengthen parties' commitment to extend beyond purely theoretical language.

The Preamble states:

"… However great the challenges may be of educating each Minneapolis student to her or his full potential, the parties to this agreement are determined to tackle them. This agreement is designed to facilitate whatever change and experiments may be needed."[35]

OTHER DISTRICT THAT HAS USED CONTRACT LANGUAGE ON STUDENT ACHIEVEMENT

- Seattle

CASE EXAMPLE:

Minneapolis Preamble Addresses Learning Gaps Between Children

MINNEAPOLIS. The 2001-2003 agreement between the Board of Education of Special School District #1 and the Minneapolis Federation of Teachers contains an extensive preamble based upon a joint commitment "to the education of the children of Minneapolis." The preamble acknowledges unacceptable learning gaps between students of color and white students and explicitly refers to challenges faced by children from impoverished and dysfunctional communities. The preamble also notes that many parents or guardians, though committed to their children's welfare, may not be able to partner with the schools on behalf of their children because they are struggling with work schedules, the difficulties of poverty, and schools that may be intimidating or "out of touch with the culture of their lives." The contract also acknowledges that teachers, too, are often badly prepared to address the needs of poor children and need help.

CHAPTER FOOTNOTES

34. Examples include the 2002-2005 Douglas County Agreement that contains a "Memorandum of Understanding Regarding Statement of Alignment," Page 64, and the 2001-2004 Toledo Agreement, Appendix X.

35. Preamble, 2001-2003. Agreement Between the Board of Education of Special School District #1 and the Minneapolis Federation of Teachers.

RESOURCES AND REFERENCES

- **Denver Public Schools**
  Andre Pettigrew, Assistant Superintendent
  for Administrative Services
  900 Grant Street, Room 402, Denver, CO 80203
  Tel: 720.423.3271   Fax: 720.423.3413
  www.dpsk12.org

- **Denver Classroom Teachers Association**
  Becky Wissink, President
  Tel: 303.831.0590   Fax: 303.831.0591
  bwissink@nea.org

- **Minneapolis Federation of Teachers**
  Louise Sundin, President
  67 8th Ave., NE, Minneapolis, MN 55413
  Tel: 612.529.9621   Fax: 612.529.0539
  www.MFT59.org
  lsundin@mft59.org

- **Minneapolis Public Schools**
  Katrina Robertson Reed, Former Human Resources Director
  ThoughtBridge Consulting Group
  3 Bow Street, Cambridge, MA 02138
  Tel: 617.868.8641   Fax: 617.868.8642
  www.thoughtbridge.net
  Robreedk@aol.com

- **Providence Teachers Union**
  Steven F. Smith, President
  99 Corliss Street, Providence, RI 02904
  Tel: 401.421.4014   Fax: 401.421.9239
  www.proteun.org
  ssmith@proteun.org

- **Providence Public Schools**
  Melody Johnson, Superintendent
  797 Westminster Street, Providence, RI 02903
  Tel: 401.456.9100   Fax: 401.456.9252

Improving the Quality of Teaching and Teachers

Improving the quality of teachers and teaching is central to the current education reform agenda. Today's intense focus on effective teaching is informed by research that clearly links the importance of high-quality teaching to the narrowing of the achievement gap between advantaged and disadvantaged children.[1] There is strong evidence that good teaching has a positive effect on student learning—in fact, it has the single largest effect on a student's potential to overcome the effect of race, poverty, or any of the other risk factors for low achievement. The clear policy conclusion of this work is that *all* children should be taught by good teachers.

Underscoring the importance of teaching quality, the federal *No Child Left Behind Act* requires "highly qualified" teachers in every Title I classroom by the end of the 2005-6 academic year.[2] States and districts are required annually to measure and report progress towards the goal to the federal government. The student achievement aims of *NCLB* as well as the requirements

for "highly qualified teachers" have caused school districts to examine and redesign their personnel policies to recruit, support, develop, and retain the best teachers.

Unprecedented teacher shortages[3] also make the issue of finding and developing "highly qualified teachers" relevant to all school districts. The vast majority of today's veteran teachers will retire in the next few years, resulting in an "experience drain" and requiring a massive recruitment, hiring, and development effort.

While new teachers are being recruited at an ever-increasing pace, it is also true that attrition of both experienced and new teachers is accelerating at a faster rate.[4] New teachers find their first years on the job extremely difficult. They lack resources and materials, including textbooks. Classroom conditions are often uncomfortable. They are overwhelmed with paperwork, feel unprepared to meet the learning needs and disciplinary issues of the children in their classrooms. They report that they are isolated in their classrooms and feel unwelcome in their schools. Teachers in high-poverty schools cite additional challenges: student and teacher absenteeism, high concentrations of English-language learners, and students reading below grade level.

Teacher turnover at current rates, whether through retirement, career change, or school transfer, is problematic for improving student achievement and closing the achievement gap between advantaged and disadvantaged students. Turnover creates a sorting mechanism whereby the most needy children are taught by the least effective teachers while advantaged students are taught by the most effective teachers. Teaching effectiveness is, in part, a function of experience: the more experienced teachers are, on average, the more effective they are in the classroom.[5] The most senior teachers have the greatest choice about where they will work, particularly in unionized districts where rules governing teaching assignments are based on seniority. All other things being equal, experienced teachers, who can, steer away from high-needs schools, moving to wealthier districts or less needy schools within their home district.[6] The openings they leave behind are filled by less senior, often new, less effective teachers. Despite the research that shows that high-need schools benefit most from effective teachers, ironically, it is these same schools that are twice as likely to be staffed with teachers who are both under-prepared in the subject areas that they teach and least experienced in teaching.[7] This pattern exists not only across school districts but within school districts as well.[8]

Turnover not only affects student achievement, it is costly as well. American schools spend between $2.1 billion and $2.6 billion cumulatively replacing teachers.[9] The cost of recruiting, hiring, and training a new teacher is estimated at 30 percent of the salary of the exiting teacher. The costs are not only monetary. Turnover requires the attention of leaders and drains other elements of organizational capacity. Constant churning in a workgroup means that a supportive professional community is less likely to form.[10] Turnover costs are compounded when a teacher leaves and a district and/or school loses the professional development investment that it has made in training this person, who is often a more effective instructor as a result of this investment.

As a result of these conditions, many of the long-standing mechanisms for preparing and distributing teachers are being redesigned, and notions about professional growth, careers, and rewards for teaching are being rethought. Some school districts, joined by their unions, are examining the operation of their human resources office and the contractual regulations concerning the hiring and assignment of teachers in order to design ways of distributing effective teachers to schools and classrooms where they are most needed. Assuring that *all* students are taught by effective teachers requires a *systemic* approach to supporting both new and experienced teachers. This approach includes meaningful supervision and evaluations, remedial help when necessary, expanded career ladders for teachers, and rewards for effective teachers.

This chapter describes a number of innovations designed and implemented by districts and unions collaboratively. Most of these innovations occur in clusters—that is to say, where you find one, you are likely to find others.[11] For example, well-designed induction and mentoring programs to support new teachers usually also offer experienced teachers new career opportunities as mentors and these new opportunities give them incentives to stay in the profession. It is also true that many of these innovations are capable of existing alone, and often, systemic change starts with the design and implementation of one small innovation.

TEACHER HIRING, ASSIGNMENT, AND TRANSFER

Placing the right teachers in the right jobs in the right schools can be difficult in a large, multi-site school system. Centralized hiring at the district level and competing criteria for assignment to specific positions often impede appropriate teacher placement. Student needs are often superseded by bureaucratic procedures or strict seniority practices. However, in many instances, school districts and unions have overcome these challenges and agreed on ways to attract good teachers and place them appropriately.

USEFULNESS TO IMPROVING STUDENT ACHIEVEMENT

Innovative hiring, assignment, and transfer practices described in this section improve the likelihood that students will be taught by an appropriately qualified teacher—a person who has been selected by people with the greatest knowledge of the school's needs and the greatest immediate interest in the teacher's qualifications, alignment with pedagogical style and goals, and teaching effectiveness.

A school's success is directly related to the quality of its teachers, their commitment to the school's mission, their comfort and fit in its culture, and their ability to work with one another and the student population. It is critical that principals and people at local school sites are given the ability and authority to select the teachers whom they judge to be the most likely to succeed in their particular settings. This is especially true as accountability is increasingly focused on schools and other small learning communities.[12]

The larger problem of cumbersome, bureaucratic procedures, coupled with poor communication between school sites and central hiring offices delays the hiring of qualified applicants. Assignment and transfer rights based on seniority create additional delays. In combination, these delays discourage applicants who then take positions elsewhere.[13]

CASE EXAMPLE:

Seattle Process Gives Great Control To Schools Over Hiring of Teachers

SEATTLE. The Seattle School District and Seattle Education Association have negotiated an extensive staffing process that gives considerable control over teacher hiring to individuals at school sites and provides the district with authority over teacher transfer. Consideration of the role of seniority is all but eliminated in the hiring and transfer processes.[14]

When hiring, individual school sites can hire from outside as well as within the school district, without giving preference to teachers already employed by the district.

Schools are able to design their own hiring process, provided that certain features are incorporated, including:

- The hiring team and principal must jointly develop criteria for staff selection. Criteria must be aligned with the school's "Academic Achievement or Transformation Plan."
- Members of hiring teams must be trained in matters involving illegal employment discrimination based on protected status such as age, race, gender, and other factors.
- Teachers returning from leave or displaced from prior positions must be considered in the hiring process.
- Interview teams must include teachers who are knowledgeable about the requirements of the Academic Achievement or Transformation Plan.
- The contract *recommends* that individual school hiring processes result in decisions that are based on consensus of principal and staff. A minimum requirement regarding staff participation is stated, and some alternate options are described.[15]

CONTRACT LANGUAGE EXAMPLES: TEACHER HIRING, ASSIGNMENT, & TRANSFER

2001-2004 Collective Bargaining Agreement Between Seattle School District No. 1 and SEA Non-Supervisory Employees. Article VIII, A and B (2-a&g).

Staffing Decisions—The District and SEA believe that staffing decisions should offer students the teachers who can best help them meet their learning goals, promote excellent teaching and allow resources to be expended where they have the highest educational value. The District and SEA also believe that school staff should have a meaningful role in the decisions that affect them.

Phase I: September 1st –July 31st: Any certified teacher or certified staff other than teachers, from within or outside of the Seattle School District (including new recruits), is eligible to be considered on the basis of his/her qualifications for any opening for which such teacher is certified.

Phase II: August 1st – August 14th (or until all displaced staff have been placed). Phase II requires that principals and building leadership teams *consider* (emphasis added) the remaining unassigned staff for openings.

2003-2006 Agreement Between the Orleans Parish School Board and United Teachers of New Orleans. Article 10:9

Schools that have not achieved their growth targets as set by the Louisiana State Department of Education and are in corrective action will be given priority in staffing the school. As such, vacancies shall not be filled in accordance with the voluntary transfer procedure or the surplusing provision of Articles 10 and 23.

Seattle also has an "administrative transfer procedure" applying to all teachers. While successful teachers may apply to any district opening for which they are certified, any teacher may be tapped by central administration for involuntary transfer at almost any time. The district has the authority to adjust staffing through involuntary transfer when the administration deems it appropriate, in order to meet district financial and educational goals. Administrative transfer decisions should be based on the premise that employee assignment has a significant impact on the employee's morale and on the effectiveness of a total educational program.[16] Teachers who are transferred by administrative decision during the school year may be given as little as one week's written notice prior to transfer, and notice shall include reasons. Teachers who are on probation cannot be transferred from one school to another without the approval of the principal and program managers of the proposed receiving transfer site.[17]

In the summer of 2004, the district and the SEA bargained additional language allowing the district, upon the agreement of the SEA, to involuntarily transfer a certified teacher without any administrative process. This language has been added to pre-existing language and does not supplant it.[18]

they do advance, they receive additional compensation, and have opportunities and responsibilities that are unique—including the required responsibility to accept assignments, which meet school or district needs regardless of individual contractual/seniority rights that might otherwise apply. Lead Teachers do have input in the assignment process, but ultimately the decisions are made by school-based planning teams and based on the overall needs of the school.[20]

Concerning transfer in Rochester, the collective-bargaining agreement authorizes the joint labor-management committee to "consider and approve" voluntary or involuntary transfer of teachers between schools in certain circumstances, without regard for the normal contractual transfer process.[21] Accordingly, Rochester school sites are able to tailor teacher staffing to program needs.

ADDITIONAL READING

- Levin, J. and Quinn, M. (2004). *Missed Opportunities: How We Keep High-Quality Teachers Out of Urban Classrooms.* New York, N.Y.: The New Teacher Project. www.tntp.org/docs/report/final/9-12/pdf

CASE EXAMPLE:

Rochester Contract Clauses Grant Flexibility in Teacher Assignments

ROCHESTER, N.Y. In Rochester, the parties have negotiated flexibility with teacher assignments through contract clauses involving career ladders and contract waivers. Rochester has a *Career in Teaching Plan* based on four career development levels for teachers.[19] The most advanced level on the career ladder is that of "Lead Teacher." Teachers are not required to move to Lead Teacher status in order to remain in good standing, but if

RESOURCES AND REFERENCES

- **Rochester Public Schools**
  Manuel J. Rivera, Superintendent
  131 West Broad Street, Rochester, NY 14614
  Tel: 585.262 8100
  www.rcsdk12.org
  manuel.rivera@rcsdk12.org

- **Rochester Teachers Association**
  Adam Urbanski, President
  30 N. Union Street, Suite 301, Rochester, NY 14607
  Tel: 585.546.2681
  www.rochesterteachers.com
  urbanski@rochesterteachers.com

- **Seattle Public Schools**
  Raj Manhas, Superintendent
  2445 3rd Avenue South, Seattle, WA 98134
  Mail to: Seattle Public Schools
  P.O. Box 34165, Seattle, WA 98124-1165
  Tel: 206.252.0000
  www.seattleschools.org
  rsmanhas@seattleschools.org

- **Seattle Education Association**
  John Dunn, President
  Nancy Murphy, Executive Director
  720 Nob Hill Avenue North, Seattle, WA 98109
  Tel: 206.283.8443

CHAPTER FOOTNOTES

1. Haycock, K. (1998) Good Teaching Matters....A lot. Washington, D.C. Education Trust.

2. Teachers of core subjects are required to be "highly qualified" by 2002-3 according to the No Child Left Behind Act.

3. Ingersoll, R.M. (2001) Teacher turnover and teacher shortages: An organizational analysis. American Education Research Journal.. 38 (3) Pp. 499-534.

4. National Commision of Teaching and America's Future. (2004) No Dream Denied: A Pledge to America's Children. Washington, D.C. Page 22.

5. E.A. Hanushek, J.F. Kain and S.G. Rivkin. "The Revolving Door." Education Next. Winter. 2004. Page 77.

6. Ibid.

7. Education Week. "To Close the Gap, Quality Counts." Jan. 9, 2003. An analysis of SASS data by Education Week found that teachers in high-poverty and high-minority schools report much more difficult working conditions on some fronts than do teachers in other schools. Also see Craig D. Gerald, "All Talk, No Action: Putting An End to Out-of-Field Teaching." The Education Trust, 2002.

8. E.A. Hanushek;, J.F. Kain; and S.G. Rivkin. "The Revolving Door." Education Next. Winter. 2004. Page 80.

9. Alliance for Excellent Education (2004) Tapping the Potential: Retaining and Developing High-Quality New Teachers. Washington, D.C. Pp. 1, 7-8.

10. National Commission on Teaching and America's Future (2004). No Dream Denied: A Pledge to America's Children. Washington, D.C.: Author. Pp. 32-35.

11. See Milgrom, P. and Roberts, J. (1995). Complementarities and fit: Strategy, structure and organization change. Journal of Accounting and Economics. 19(2-3):179-208; Holmstrom, B. and Milgrom, P. (1994). The firm as an incentive system. American Economic Review. 84(4):972-91.

12. On a related note, a recent Massachusetts Supreme Judicial Court tested the authority of the principal in Beverly to terminate a sixth grade teacher who had been accused of physically and verbally abusing his students on multiple occasions. In weighing the merits of the case and reviewing the purpose of the state's 1993 Education Reform Act (MERA), the court observed that the state's teacher dismissal statute is not only about the relationship between employer and employee, it is about the education of students. School District of Beverly v. Geller. Suffolk. April 2 — Oct. 5, 2001. Indeed, Chapter 71, Section 42 of Title XII, Education, includes "inefficiency," "incompetence," "incapacity," and other grounds for termination of teachers. Significantly, the statute states that in deciding a teacher's appeal of dismissal, an arbitrator "shall consider the best interest of the pupils in the district and the need for elevation of performance standards." MGL-Chapter 71, Section 42.

13. Levin, J. and Quinn, M. (2004). Missed Opportunities: How We Keep High-Quality Teachers Out of Urban Classrooms. New York, N.Y.: The New Teacher Project.

14. Seniority remains a factor in layoff (staff adjustment/displacement) under the agreement. Article VIII-Bf.

15. 2001-2004 Collective Bargaining Agreement between Seattle School District No. 1 and SEA Certified Non-Supervisory Employees, Article VIII-3.

16. 2001-2004 Collective Bargaining Agreement between Seattle School District No. 1 and SEA Certified Non-Supervisory Employees, Article IX E-1.

17. 2001-2004 Collective Bargaining Agreement between Seattle School District No. 1 and SEA Certified Non-Supervisory Employees, Section IX E-2e.

18. Dec. 9, 2004, correspondence, Bill Bleakney, Executive Director of Human Resources, Seattle Public Schools.

19. July 1, 2002, contract between the City School District of Rochester and the Rochester Teachers Association, Section 52-1.

20. Ibid. Section 52-12f-1.

21. Ibid. Section 51.

PROFESSIONAL DEVELOPMENT

Collaboratively designed professional development programs represent joint efforts of teachers' unions and districts to improve student outcomes by improving the quality of instruction. Such programs include comprehensive orientation and induction programs for new teachers, personal mentors, ongoing training, and expanded opportunities beyond classroom teaching for experienced teachers.

Innovative professional development programs described here seek to minimize strong disincentives—such as inadequate preparation, isolated struggle, obsolete skills, and a dead-end career track—that dissuade teachers from remaining in the profession. New and veteran teachers, like other professionals, need continuing education in their field. The challenges presented by new student populations, curriculum standards, and high-stakes accountability require fresh approaches, new skills, and support.

USEFULNESS TO IMPROVING STUDENT ACHIEVEMENT

Continuing professional development prepares and supports new teachers and helps experienced teachers face new teaching challenges. Providing teachers with the professional skills and support they need to succeed in their job improves teaching quality, increases job satisfaction, reduces stress, and aids retention of effective teachers. Higher-quality teachers lead to improved student learning.

Programs discussed here depart from traditional professional development because they are not imposed unilaterally by the administration, but have arisen through district-union collaboration. As a result of this partnership, they address the perspective and concerns of classroom teachers rather than just those of administrator organizers. Teachers' primary criticism of most professional development has been that they "have long been subjected to in-service sessions that are offered sporadically, based on the latest education fad, and often delivered by 'outside experts'...with little impact on classroom practice."[22]

When the union is a prominent sponsor, co-sponsor, or provider of these activities, it has an incentive to satisfy its members. School district co-sponsorship acts as an additional check on quality and relevance. The union sees these activities as a service to its members, thereby increasing the value of membership, focusing on improving professional practice and strengthening the union as an organization. The district and the union are aligned in their interests about professional development, and this alignment can be useful to the larger goals of improving student achievement.

Collective-bargaining agreements in several districts establish a variety of jointly designed and implemented professional development programs for new and experienced teachers, including:

- New teacher development and mentorship programs, sometimes called "induction" programs that integrate teachers into school life, providing up to a yearlong mentoring relationship with an experienced teacher for continuing support.[23]
- Teacher academies or institutes offering training and support on topics related to teaching and instruction such as testing and diagnostic skills, classroom management, learning disabilities, least restrictive alternative placement, etc.[27]
- Career ladders where teachers progress from lower to higher levels based on criteria other than straight seniority.[28] Teachers with advanced status on career ladders often have responsibilities

INDUCTION WORKS

Induction has been shown to be cost effective, returning $1.37 in value for every dollar spent while reducing the time it takes a new teacher to become effective.[24] Teachers who participated in an active induction program have been found to increase the language and math achievement of their students by an additional half-year over teachers in less engaging programs, in part counteracting some of the negative effects of socio-economic status, or English-language learner or disability status.[25] Districts with union-district induction programs have seen attrition of new teachers decline by two-thirds.[26]

beyond teaching, such as mentoring new teachers.

- Externships, allowing teachers time to develop content knowledge, teaching skills, and broadened perspectives.[29]
- Professional leave banks that operate like sick leave banks, permitting teachers to take time from their regular duties to pursue professional development opportunities.[30]
- Educational issues forums providing opportunities to explore specific topic areas through lectures by outside experts, and discussion.[31]

CASE EXAMPLE:

N.Y.C. Contract Language Requires Support Services for New Teachers

NEW YORK, N.Y. The New York City Schools' contract requires that new, incoming teachers receive professional support when they commence service. Primary components of the district's professional development plan include the new teacher staff development and mentor teacher internships.[32]

The new teacher staff development program requires that teachers partake in between three and 10 days of professional development activities during their first year, with the length of time depending upon certification status and prior experience. The content and design of professional development programs is developed collaboratively by the union and the district, taking into account the different needs of individual teachers as a result of their educational and professional backgrounds. Teachers are paid for days spent in professional development activities.

The mentor teacher internship program pairs new, non-certified teachers with experienced teachers who are selected by a committee, the majority of whose members are teachers. Mentors must be experienced teachers with demonstrable knowledge of policies, performance standards, subject matter, and mastery of pedagogical skills. Mentors are released from all teaching duties. Time for mentor-teacher interaction is provided to teachers. Communications between the mentors and the teacher are confidential, and neither is evaluated with respect to the relationship. District and union representatives have developed a professional development program for mentors.[33] The assignment is renewable after one year subject to re-application.

Beginning in September 2004, 36 new positions for "lead teachers" were created in eight elementary schools and in one K-8 school in the Bronx, as the result of work by a coalition of parent and community groups with the UFT and the New York Board of Education.[34] The teachers in these positions spend half of the day teaching children (sharing the class with another lead teacher), opening their classroom to other teachers as a lab. The remainder of the day is spent mentoring other teachers through modeling best practices, coaching, and leading study groups. They receive a salary increase of $10,000 for these new responsibilities. Lead teachers must have five years teaching experience, outstanding classroom

abilities, and be vetted through two selection committees. The first committee serves as a regional personnel committee qualifying applicants. The second committee, which is based in the participating school and includes a majority of teachers, as well as parents and administrators, selects from among the qualified applicants. The principal has the right to veto the selections.

CASE EXAMPLE:

Miami-Dade Launches Tracks, Innovative Programs for Teachers

MIAMI-DADE COUNTY. The 2003-2006 contract between the Miami-Dade County Public Schools and the United Teachers of Dade describes a multi-faceted approach to "improve schools and student achievement by raising the status of the education profession and increasing parental involvement." Parties state their commitment "to collaborate in creating innovative models for training teachers, substitutes, and paraprofessionals, making full use of modern technology."[35] The contract describes a number of unique professional development programs, including POP (the Professional Opportunity Program), DATA (Dade Academy for the Teaching Arts), and others.

POP provides teachers opportunities to work in capacities other than full-time classroom teaching—positions referred to as "tracks." Tracks are jointly created by the parties and are offered to qualified teachers who apply and succeed in a jointly administered, multi-stepped, rigorous selection process. Track appointments are for a minimum of one year, with continuation dependent upon evaluation results.

Examples of tracks include:

- Resident teacher positions in the Dade Academy for Teaching Arts—a professional growth academy for teachers in the district;

- Teacher-coordinator positions in the district's bilingual vocational instruction program; and
- Peer intervention and assistance from consulting teachers, who work with new and struggling teachers.

Tracks generally offer additional compensation, in accordance with the district's negotiated pay schedule. They also provide variety, exposure, and other incentives as agreed upon by the parties.[36]

Dade Academy for the Teaching Arts (DATA) was established by the parties to stimulate teachers' professional growth. Its stated objectives include updating and expanding content/subject-area knowledge, broadening professional perspectives, and refining instructional skills. "Enrollment" in DATA involves a mini-sabbatical of nine weeks, designed to "energize, revitalize, and enhance the professionalization of teachers." Participating teachers are free of home school responsibilities during their nine-week assignment and are guaranteed the right to return to all previously assigned assignments and positions upon return to their home school.[37]

In addition to the POP and DATA programs, Dade County has several other professional development resources, including:

- **Educational Issues Forum.** The district has agreed to fund educational issues forum grants to give teachers the opportunity to hear inspirational speakers and to plan their own seminars, colloquia, and other speaking events.[38]
- **Professional Leave Bank.** The parties have created a professional leave bank that allows teachers to deposit and withdraw time credit in order to facilitate attendance at professional development events and programs.[39]
- **Sabbatical Leaves.** The parties have agreed to explore a sabbatical leave program for teachers.[40]

CASE EXAMPLE:

Minn. Centers Designed to Promote 'Site-Based' Professional Development

MINNEAPOLIS. The Minneapolis Board of Education and Minneapolis Federation of Teachers have jointly developed Professional Development Centers (PDCs). The centers are described in the collective-bargaining agreement as "a collaborative effort of school sites, Minneapolis Public Schools, Minneapolis Federation of Teachers and Teacher Instructional Services to promote teacher quality and enhance student achievement."[41] Centers are spread throughout the district in multiple sites, serving single schools or small clusters of schools. Their purpose is "to promote continuous, site-based, job-embedded professional development that supports/enriches the skills of staff, parents, students, and the school community. They provide a forum for reflecting on educational reforms, teaching practice, student needs, and family/community involvement."[42]

Stated objectives of the PDCs are to:

- Analyze and use student data;
- Align their efforts with the 'District Improvement Agenda' (DIA);
- Foster and maintain professional networks;
- Provide access to research; and
- Remain accountable for documenting the link between high-quality professional development and student achievement.[43]

Union-Sponsored Professional Development

Increasingly, national unions and state and local affiliates are providing or supplementing professional development. They are collaborating with school districts, higher education institutions, foundations, and research groups to become professional development service providers.[44] This work was demonstrated by the

American Federation of Teachers (AFT) when it passed a resolution on Union-Sponsored Professional Development in 2002.[45] In so doing, it recognized the importance of professional development to professional success and stated a number of ways that local unions could assist in the process of improving professional development opportunities for members. AFT-recommended strategies included brokering, collaboration, and delivery.

Brokering is using the influence of state and local union leaders to leverage existing professional development programs by forging relationships with outside organizations, such as universities, that already offer such training.

- In New York, the United Federation of Teachers (UFT) Teacher Center offers 150 courses each semester that can be applied toward master's degrees at local colleges.
- The Minneapolis program began as a partnership between the union, district, and the University of Minnesota College of Education and Human Development, supported by grants from the union and the State of Minnesota Board of Teaching.[46]

Collaboration is working with partners, including employers, to increase professional development offerings.[47] The case examples discussed in detail above are collaborative efforts. Many of these local programs are supported, in part, by AFT-run, national-level professional development training programs, such as: Educational Research and Dissemination (ER&D) and Quality Educational Standards in Teaching (QuEST). The ER&D effort develops the capacity in locals, often in partnership with school districts, to design and deliver high-quality professional development to their members. ER&D has 12 instructional strands, all based on educational research and translated for use in classroom practice. The strands include Reading, Thinking Math, Managing Anti-Social Behavior, the

CONTRACT LANGUAGE EXAMPLES: PROFESSIONAL DEVELOPMENT

2000-2003 Agreement Between The Board of Education of the City School District of the City of New York and The United Federation of Teachers. Article 8G

The content and design of this professional development program for new teachers shall be developed collaboratively by the union and the Board and will take into account the varying needs of new teachers based on their educational and professional backgrounds. As an educational option the Board and the union agree to develop criteria for college courses that can be credited toward fulfillment of the first year professional development requirement in order to coordinate services and requirements for new teachers.

As one aspect of the parties' interest in professional development, a joint Board-Union committee comprised of three (3) designees of the UFT President and three (3) designees of the Chancellor was established to expand and professionalize available staff development opportunities.

Home-School Connection, Foundations of Effective Teaching, and Instructional Strategies that Work. To date, ER&D has worked in 200 locals.

Additionally, on the national level AFT holds a biennial QuEST conference, in Washington, D.C., open to teams of teachers and administrators from affiliated districts.[48] The union encourages large, diverse teams, giving registration fee relief to teachers younger than 35 years of age and to administrators and school board members. The conference provides support in a variety of ways to districts that are taking a team approach to improving student achievement. Mini pre-conference institutes address reading and math learning, while conference workshops address

Memorandum of Agreement: Lead Teacher Pilot Project. Between Board of Education of the City of New York and the United Federation of Teachers.

4. In the elementary schools, each pair of lead teachers will have responsibility for one regular class. Each lead teacher will be programmed for a duty-free lunch period and a preparation period that will be scheduled at the same time as the preparation period of the lead teacher with whom they are sharing a class. Half of the remainder of the day will be spent teaching their class and half providing professional support to teaching staff.

5. Intermediate School lead teachers will be programmed for a duty free lunch and a preparation period each day. Lead teachers will teach three regular classes per day and will provide professional support to teaching staff three periods per day.

Miami-Dade County Public Schools, United Teachers of Dade, 2003-2006 Successor Contract.

The parties reaffirm their commitment to educational excellence and improvement of the overall quality of instruction by attracting and retaining superior teachers through establishment of a system of career advancement based upon superior performance, professional growth and development, and economic incentives... (Article XXVI, Section 6 (A)).

... Accordingly, the MDCPS Professional Opportunities Program has been established as a horizontal career ladder consisting of multiple and varied professional opportunities ("tracks") for teachers. MDCPS POP incorporates specific career opportunities previously agreed to by the parties as joint professionalization of teaching/education initiatives...(Article XXVI, Section 6(B)).

The Dade Academy for the Teaching Arts (DATA) has been established for the purpose of stimulating professional growth. DATA provides teachers with the opportunity to participate in a planned program of seminars, clinics, externships, and independent study. Its major objectives are to: update and expand content/subject area knowledge, broaden professional perspectives, and refine and enhance instructional skills. The parties encourage participation in the DATA program by eligible teachers and agree to pursue making this opportunity available to elementary, as well as secondary level teachers, subject to available funding. (Article XXVI, Section 7.)

policy areas such as IDEA and Redesigning Schools to Raise Student Achievement.

The third strategy, direct service delivery includes:

- In Pittsburgh, the local union stepped in to provide support during the early 1990s, when the district significantly reduced its financial support of professional development for teachers. The union's ER&D (Education Research and Development) program filled the void. The membership voted to provide funds to maintain and expand the ER&D program. Since then, the program has evolved into a partnership with both parties contributing time and resources to offer courses to large numbers of district teachers.[49]

- The Chicago Teachers Union, with the support of the MacArthur Foundation, launched a QuEST Center providing a range of professional development services from basic classroom management, preparation for National Board Certification, and consultation on small school design.[50]

OTHER EXAMPLES OF DISTRICTS WITH INNOVATIVE PROFESSIONAL DEVELOPMENT PRACTICES

- Albuquerque, N.Mex.
- Chicago
- Cincinnati
- Columbus, Ohio

RESOURCES AND REFERENCES

- **American Federation of Teachers**
  Linda Stelly, AFT Project Manager,
  QuEST Program
  555 New Jersey Ave. NW, Washington, DC 20001
  Tel: 202.879.4400
  www.aft.org/quest

- **American Federation of Teachers**
  Rob Weil, Director
  Educational Research and Dissemination
  (ER&D) Program
  Deputy Director, AFT Educational Issues Department
  555 New Jersey Ave. NW, Washington, DC 20001
  Tel: 800.238.1133 x6953
  www.aft.org/topics/teacher-quality/erd.htm
  rweil@aft.org

- **Chicago Teachers Union**
  Allen Bearden, QuEST Center
  Carlene Lutz, QuEST Center Coordinator
  222 Merchandise Mart Plaza, Suite 400
  Chicago, IL 60654-1016
  Tel: 312.329.9100   Fax: 312.329.6205
  www.ctunet.com
  AllenBearden@ctulocall.com
  CarleneLutz@ctulocal1.com

CHAPTER FOOTNOTES

22. American Federation of Teachers. *Educational Research Dissemination Program.* What Makes ER&D Different. www.aft.org

23. New York, N.Y., and Wichita, Kan.

24. Villar, A. (2004). *Measuring the benefits and costs of mentor-based induction: A value-added assessment of new teacher effectiveness linked to student achievement.* Santa Cruz, Calif.A: New Teacher Center.

25. Thompson, M., Paek, P. Goe, L. Ponte, E. (2004) *Research summary: Study of the impact of the California formative assessment and support system for teachers.* Princeton, N.J.: Educational Testing Service. Similar results have been shown in Rochester, N.Y. See McGowan, A. (2000). *Policy perspective: Evidence of significantly positive effects of the RCSD mentor program.* Rochester, N.Y.: Rochester City School District, Department of Research, Education, Testing and Records.

26. National Commission on Teaching and America's Future. (1996). *What Matters Most: Teaching for America's Future.* New York, N.Y.: Teachers College, Columbia University.

27. Toledo, Ohio; Dade County, Fla.; Seattle; Montgomery County, Md.; Pinellas County, Fla.

28. 2000-2003 Agreement between Cincinnati Federation of Teachers and Cincinnati Board of Education. Section 170.; Rochester, N.Y. See July 1, 2002, contract between the City School District of Rochester and the Rochester Teachers Association, Section 52.

29. 1999-2000 Contract Between Miami-Dade Public Schools and United Teachers of Dade. Article XXVI, Section 7.

30. Ibid. Section 9.

31. Ibid. Section 13.

32. 2000-2003 Agreement Between the Board of Education of the City School District of the City of New York and the United Federation of Teachers. Article 8G.

33. The job posting for full-time mentors, including selection criteria, duties, and responsibilities can be found at www.nycenet.edu.

34. Herszenhorn, D.M. In pilot project, a new role for teachers. *The New York Times.* June 15, 2004. Community groups include ACORN, Citizens Advice Bureau, Highbridge Community Life Center, Mid-Bronx Council, New Settlement Apartments, Northwest Brox Community and Clergy Coalition, and is supported by New York University Institute for Education and Social Policy.

35. 1999-2002 contract between the Miami Dade County Public Schools and the United Teachers of Dade, Article XXVI, Preamble.

36. Ibid. Article XXVI, Section 6.

37. Ibid. Article XXVI, Section 7.

38. Ibid. Article XXVI, Section 13.

39. Ibid. Article XXVI, Section 9.

40. Ibid. Article XXVI, Section 9.

41. 2003-2005 Agreement between the Minneapolis Board of Education and the Minneapolis Federation of Teachers, Article V. Section N. Page 109.

42. Ibid.

43. Ibid.

44. AFT. *Professional Development: It's Union Work.* 2000. Page 5.

45. www.aft.org/about/resolutions/2002/prof_dev.html

46. U.S. Department of Education. National Conference on Teacher Quality. *Exemplary Practices for Mentoring New Teachers.* www.ed.gov/inits/teachers/exemplarypractices.

47. AFT Resolutions: 2002. www.aft.org/about/resolutions/2002/prof_dev.html

48. American Federation of Teachers. *Quality Educational Standards in Teaching (QuEST).* www.aft.org/QuEST2003.

49. American Federation of Teachers. Professional Development: It's Union Work. 2000. Page. 8.

50. Chicago Teachers Union. www.ctunet.com/quest

- **Chicago Public Schools**
Arne Duncan, Chief Executive Officer
Barbara Eason-Watkins, Chief Education Officer
Central Office
125 S. Clark Street, 6th Floor, Chicago, IL 60603
Tel: 773.553.1000   Fax: 773.553.1601
http://www.cps.k12.il.us/
aduncan@cps.k12.il.us
bewatkins@cps.k12.il.us

- **Miami-Dade County Public Schools**
Rudolph F. Crew, Superintendent
1450 NE Second Ave., Miami, FL 33132
Tel: 305.995.1430   Fax: 305.995.1000
www.dadeschools.net

- **United Teachers of Dade**
Karen Aronowitz, President
2200 Biscayne Blvd., Miami, FL 33137
Tel: 305.854.0220, Ext. 244
www.utd.org
karena@utofd.com

- **Minneapolis Federation of Teachers**
Louise Sundin, President
67 8th Ave., NE, Minneapolis, MN 55413
Tel: 612.529.9621   Fax: 612.529.0539
www.MFT59.org

- **University of Minnesota**
Patricia Thornton, Coordinator of Teacher Development,
Curriculum and Instruction
125 Peik Hall 159 Pillsbury Dr. SE, Minneapolis, MN 55455
Tel: 612.626.8974   Fax: 612.624.8744
thorn020@umn.edu

- **New York City Board of Education**
Division of Human Resources Center for Recruitment and
Professional Development
65 Court Street, Brooklyn, NY 11201
www.nycenet.edu

- **New York City Board of Education**
Yvonne Torres, Community Superintendent
District 9, Region 1
One Fordham Plaza 8th Floor, Bronx, N.Y. 10458
Tel : 718.741.7071
www.nycenet.edu
CC9LeadTeacher@yahoo.com

- **New York City United Federation of Teachers**
Randi Weingarten, President
52 Broadway Avenue, New York, NY 10004
Tel: 212.777.7500
www.uft.org

- **New York City United Federation of Teachers**
Esta Heither UFT Teacher Center
Coordinator for New Teacher Development
Tel: 718.935.4463

- **New York City United Federation of Teachers**
Marilyn Chadwick, Peer Intervention Program Coordinator
Tel: 212.844.0585
PIP@UFT.org

- **Strengthening and Sustaining Teachers**
Sharon Dorsey Staff, College of Education
University of Washington, Box 353600
Seattle, WA 98195-3600
Tel: 206.616.4805
sdorsey@columbusrr.com

PEER REVIEW AND ASSISTANCE

Peer review and assistance programs offer one-on-one mentoring to new and struggling, experienced teachers. Typically, expert peers are released from classroom responsibilities to conduct multiple observations, identify areas of practice that need improvement, and help teachers develop pedagogic skills. Often, the continuation of a teacher's contract may depend on his/her progress in the peer review and assistance program.

In addition to improving teaching and retention, peer review and assistance programs address the costs and delays associated with termination of ineffective teachers. Evidence is mounting that peer review and assistance programs address this concern, while simultaneously creating a culture of professional accountability for performance.[51]

USEFULNESS TO IMPROVING STUDENT ACHIEVEMENT

Peer review and assistance programs directly address three issues that are central to improving student achievement: increasing the effectiveness of new teachers, improving the skills of struggling teachers, and retaining experienced teachers.

Unlike typical teacher evaluations, which are conducted unilaterally by principals, peer review and intervention are collaborative processes in which teachers and unions actively participate. Joint committees are formed to create, implement, and manage programs for teacher evaluation, intervention, and assistance. Often, either principals and/or union members are able to initiate the process of performance review for individual teachers, who are perceived to be in need of improvement. Struggling teachers can also request intervention on their own behalf, and sometimes win a grace period from the regular cycle of performance evaluation while they participate in an intervention program. Experienced teachers are typically selected on a competitive basis to become mentors. Peer assistant coaches are usually relieved of other teaching duties while they serve as mentors (which may be for several years), and then return to teaching.

Many have sanctioned peer review and assistance, though not all states and districts encounter circumstances that enable this type of practice. Both the National Education Association (NEA) and the American Federation of Teachers (AFT) have passed resolutions at their national conventions endorsing peer review and assistance. California has made peer evaluation mandatory in all school districts. On the other hand, state laws may indirectly preclude peer review programs or create program parameters by dictating specific processes and/or standards for the evaluation and/or termination of teachers.

CASE EXAMPLE:

Pioneering 'Toledo Plan' Stresses Peer Evaluation, Shared Decisions

TOLEDO, OHIO.[52] In 1981, the Toledo Public Schools and the Toledo Federation of Teachers pioneered a collaborative intervention and assistance program, giving teachers the authority to evaluate their peers and the responsibility to recommend their dismissal, when appropriate. The program has continued without interruption except during the 1995-1996 academic year when it was suspended during contentious negotiations. The program, widely known as "The Toledo Plan," involves peer review, evaluation (by peers and later by principals), intervention—when necessary, and eventually termination—when warranted. It is based on the premise that a collaborative decision regarding teacher quality is always better than a

unilateral one, and that great teachers possess the expertise needed to effectively assess and assist both entry-level teachers and those veteran teachers who are experiencing difficulty in the classroom.[53] The Toledo Federation of Teachers is of the view that it ought to be defending standards of performance instead of members who are unable to meet them.[54]

The Toledo Plan is administered by a nine-member Intern Board of Review panel (IBoR), consisting of four administrators and five teacher representatives, with the chair rotating annually between the president of the Toledo Federation of Teachers, and an assistant superintendent. The IBoR panel assigns and monitors consulting teachers, manages the budget, supervises professional development activities, and ultimately recommends to the superintendent the retention or termination of teachers.

Peer review and assistance under the Toledo Plan rely heavily on excellent teachers to serve as assessors, mentors, and coaches. In Toledo, this position is called the Consulting Teacher. Consulting Teachers are selected from among applicants in a competitive application process involving close scrutiny of their teaching prowess and references from peer teachers and administrators. Criteria for selection include at least five years of teaching excellence, school leadership, self-confidence, classroom management, demeanor under stress, creativity, and contribution to solutions to school management issues. Aspiring administrators are considered poor candidates. Consulting Teachers serve an apprenticeship before they begin their duties, receiving a variety of professional development opportunities. When they begin active duty, they are relieved of all teaching duties, receive additional salary, and are moved to an office shared with other consultants. They attend meetings of the IBoR panel, where they make regular reports and recommendations regarding the status of each teacher under review. A consulting teacher has a typical caseload of 10 to 12 teachers. After three years serving in the mentor role, consulting teachers are required to return to classroom teaching.

Peer Review of New Teachers. In Toledo, new teachers are hired on probationary status with one-year contracts and possible renewal for a second year. The first year is called the "intern year." Every new teacher without previous experience in the Toledo Public School system must participate in peer assistance and review during the first

teaching year and is assigned to a consulting teacher. New teachers who have prior teaching experience may be removed from the program, if approved by their consulting teacher.

During the intern year, consulting teachers are responsible for both mentoring and evaluation. They must present full evaluations of each intern's performance to the IBoR panel at the end of the first and second semesters of teaching. The second semester evaluation must contain a recommendation as to whether a teacher should be

---

CONTRACT LANGUAGE EXAMPLES: PEER REVIEW AND ASSISTANCE

2001-2004 Agreement Between The Toledo Federation of Teachers and The Toledo Public Schools. Article VIII F.

Note: The Toledo Plan has its roots in the contractual relationship between the district and the union but the parties have made a conscious decision not to bargain the fine points of the plan. In 1981, beginnings were tentative, and trust levels unstable. "The time frame and tensions of the bargaining table do not lend themselves to exploring the unknown."[59] Accordingly, the union and the district agreed in the contract only to proceed. The current agreement states that matters regarding teacher evaluation will be governed by The Toledo Plan.[60]

July 1, 2002 Contractual Agreement Between The City School District of Rochester, New York and the Rochester Teachers Association, Section 53.

Section 52 of the Rochester collective bargaining agreement describes the district's 'Career In Teaching Plan.' One component is an 'Intervention, Remediation

and Professional Support' program, presented in Section 53. The introductory language to Section 53 is as follows:

- The Intervention and Remediation component of the CIT Plan is designed to offer all available resources to help improve the performance of experienced teachers who are having serious difficulties in the performance of their professional duties.

- A teacher can be recommended in writing for Intervention and Remediation by a building principal, other appropriate supervisor or teacher constituency of the School-based Planning Team meeting as a separate group. Such written recommendation is appropriate when a teacher's performance is less than satisfactory. It is expected that such recommendation shall be initiated after reasonable efforts have been made to assist the teacher. The referral for Intervention and Recommendation may contain a recommendation as to a plan for remediation and indicate whether a withhold of all or part of the total next salary increase or any other action is warranted."

Section 53 continues through 13 additional sub-sections describing the role of a CIT panel, and the rights and responsibilities of the teacher.

hired for a second year. Evaluations are standards-based and address four performance categories: teaching procedures, classroom management, knowledge of subject-academic preparation, and work style.

Principals and other administrators are encouraged to stay out of the evaluation process altogether during the first year. They are informed about a teacher's progress by the consulting teacher and have the opportunity to inform the consultant about those aspects of performance that the consultant wouldn't necessarily be aware of, such as compliance with school policies and communications with parents. On the other hand, it is *principals* who are solely responsible for evaluation of every new teacher during the second probationary year. However, the process and criteria for evaluation do not change from year one to year two of probation.

Peer Review to Intervene with Veteran Teachers.
The intervention process under the Toledo Plan addresses performance deficiencies of experienced teachers on non-probationary contracts (traditionally known as "tenured" teachers). Veteran teachers who exhibit instructional deficiencies are referred by either the principal or the school building union committee, or both, to the IBoR panel for performance evaluation.[55] After a teacher is informed of the referral, the IBoR panel appoints an active consulting teacher to observe the teacher and recommend whether some level of intervention is warranted. There is an appeals process available to the teacher found in need of intervention, if he/she disagrees with the finding. The process allows for a third-party review by an attorney, acting as arbitrator. However, unlike some districts, Toledo does not permit a teacher to refuse intervention once the appeals process is complete.[56]

Interventions typically proceed for one to two school years during which the teacher and consultant meet regularly to set performance goals, develop a professional development plan, and review progress. Interventions end when a consultant determines that a teacher has improved and performance standards are being met, or when the consultant determines that the teacher is not making progress toward proficiency. In either case, the consultant makes no explicit recommendation concerning future employment but writes up a status report explaining why the intervention has ended. This report is submitted separately to the management representative on the IBoR panel and to the union president.

If an intervention concludes because the consulting teacher determines that progress was not made, the union has dual responsibilities—one to the peer review and assistance process and another to its member, who has a right to union representation in a termination proceeding. The union must first decide whether it agrees with the consulting teacher's decision to end intervention for lack of progress. If the union does not agree, it must decide whether it will represent the teacher in a termination proceeding. The union must assess the fairness, thoroughness, and accuracy of the consulting teacher's report and protect the right of the teacher to be treated fairly. Significantly, the union does not assume an automatic duty to represent any teacher subject to termination proceedings.

Termination decisions are ultimately made by the IBoR panel, which votes to accept or reject the recommendation of the Consulting Teacher. A simple majority is required to accept the recommendation of a Consulting Teacher to renew or terminate a teacher. Since the IBoR panel always consists of five teachers and four administrators, termination requires the votes of both administrators and union representatives. Several veteran teachers have challenged the Toledo Plan before the Ohio State Employee Relations Board and state courts where their terminations were upheld.

Impact of the Toledo Plan. The Toledo Plan has produced results that are measurable. In the five years prior to the implementation of the Toledo Plan, no veteran teachers were terminated. Today,

Toledo proportionately fires more veteran teachers than any other school district in Ohio with virtually no associated litigation costs. New teacher retention after three years is higher in Toledo than in comparable urban districts. While the Toledo Plan has associated costs, savings in terms of retention and litigation more than pay for the program.[57]

The Toledo Plan also produces less tangible outcomes. Standards-based assessment requires that teachers and administrators be able to articulate the attributes of good teaching. Teachers are expected to know and to assume responsibility for identifying and assisting teachers who need help, creating a culture of professional accountability for teaching quality.

CASE EXAMPLE:

Peer Intervention Program Targets Struggling Teachers in N.Y.C.

NEW YORK, N.Y. In New York City, the United Federation of Teachers operates the Peer Intervention Program (PIP) for tenured teachers/guidance counselors, who are struggling and nominate themselves as candidates for intervention. Established in collaboration with the New York Board of Education in 1987, the goal was to increase the effectiveness of teachers or help them transition out of the classroom to pursue other careers in public education or different industries. Teachers who receive formal warnings from their principals are typical participants, but others nominate themselves as well.[58] Assistance is given on a confidential basis and is personalized. Each teacher is assigned an intervenor who is an expert in the participant's field, and together they analyze the teacher's shortcomings, create a development plan, and establish criteria for evaluation. PIP reports that 70 percent of teachers have improved their practice as a result of peer intervention and 15 percent have left teaching. PIP uses student outcomes to measure increases in teacher effectiveness.

OTHER EXAMPLES OF DISTRICTS
USING PEER ASSISTANCE AND REVIEW

- Cincinnati
- Columbus, Ohio
- Minneapolis
- Seattle

RESOURCES AND REFERENCES

- **Rochester Public Schools**
  Manuel J. Rivera, Superintendent
  131 West Broad Street, Rochester, NY 14614
  Tel: 585.262 8100
  www.rcsdk12.org
  manuel.rivera@rcsdk12.org

- **Rochester Teachers Association**
  Adam Urbanski, President
  30 N. Union Street, Suite 301, Rochester, NY 14607
  Tel: 585.546.2681
  www.rochesterteachers.com
  urbanski@rochesterteachers.com

- **Toledo Federation of Teachers**
  Francine Lawrence, President
  111 S. Byrne Road, Toledo, OH 43615
  Tel: 419.535.3013   Fax: 419.535.0478
  www.tft.org

- **Toledo Public Schools**
  Craig Cotner, Chief Academic Officer
  420 E. Manhattan Blvd., Toledo, OH 43608
  Tel: 419.729.8422
  www.tps.org
  craig.cotner@tps.org

CHAPTER FOOTNOTES

51. See Cazares, L. and Harris, A., (2002). *Professionalism through collaboration: A social cost-benefit analysis of the Toledo Plan.* Kennedy School of Government unpublished policy analysis exercise.

52. While many articles have been written about the Toledo Plan, the most concise set of facts about the plan is available in booklet form: *The Toledo Plan, Practical Advice for Beginners.* This booklet and an accompanying compact disk were published jointly by the Toledo Federation of Teachers and the Toledo Public Schools with funds from the Kennedy School of Government Ford Innovations Award and are available to unions and districts considering a peer assessment program on the Web at http://www.tft250.org/peer_review.htm

53. Sanders, E.T.W., Superintendent, Toledo Schools (2001). *The Toledo Plan.* Published by Toledo Public Schools and Toledo Federation of Teachers. Page 4.

54. Sanders, E.T.W., Superintendent, Toledo Schools (2001). *The Toledo Plan.* Published by Toledo Public Schools and Toledo Federation of Teachers. Page 9.

55. Union votes to refer a teacher to the IBoR panel are conducted by secret ballot.

56. Rochester makes intervention a choice. See *The Toledo Plan,* Page 43.

57. See Cazares, L. and Harris, A., (2002). *Professionalism through collaboration: A social cost-benefit analysis of the Toledo Plan.* Kennedy School of Government unpublished policy analysis exercise.

58. Unwillingness to ask for peer intervention may be used by the principal as demonstrating unwillingness to address performance shortcomings in subsequent disciplinary actions.

PAY FOR PERFORMANCE

Pay-for-performance programs tie teachers' pay rates to the attainment of instructional goals by the teacher, instead of merely linking compensation with seniority and degree status. Pay-for-performance programs enhance compensation when student achievement improves. Teacher compensation may be determined on the basis of class, grade, or school-wide performance.

In addition to pay-for-performance programs, there are different forms of teacher compensation programs recognizing differentiated skill, knowledge, and responsibility. In some cases, differential compensation is available for "hard to fill" positions or especially challenging assignments.

USEFULNESS TO IMPROVING STUDENT ACHIEVEMENT

In an age of high-stakes accountability, pay-for-performance programs provide teachers an additional incentive to improve student achievement. With these programs, professional career ladders for educators are enhanced, and effective teachers have an additional way to increase their compensation—factors which make teachers less likely to leave the profession, thus reducing the negative effects of turnover. Differential pay for performance, skill, knowledge, and/or responsibility allows teachers to be rewarded for their particular contributions to student achievement.

Rewarding teachers with differentiated skill sets and whose students attain desired learning goals addresses the fundamental incentive problem created by union pay scales: that all teachers with similar status receive the same pay. Economists call this the "free rider" problem. Historically, teacher effectiveness was difficult to measure, so unions fought for standardized pay scales to assure that discrimination and favoritism did not determine pay. With the improvement in measurement methods and data collection, teaching effectiveness is more easily assessed and can now be rewarded.

While pay-for-performance programs vary in design, they all must define the desired performance measures and the method by which performance will be gauged. Performance measures can be limited to test results, or they can be expanded to include other student outcomes, such as: the percentage of students expected to perform at the next grade level without additional support, progress/growth of cohort groups over a two- to three-year period, feedback from receiving schools, evidence of teacher connection and outreach to student and families, among others. Similarly, distribution of performance awards also varies. Additional compensation can be rewarded to individual teachers and/or groups of teachers identified by team, school, or other small learning community.

Pay for performance is not a new strategy within the education field or school settings. As a result, there is considerable knowledge of and experience with the design and implementation of these plans.[61]

A consensus on design issues has emerged that informs future plans:

- Program must be developed mutually by educators, union representatives, administrators, and school board members.
- Performance awards do not make up for inadequate base salaries.
- The award must be at least between $1,000 and $3,000 in order to be meaningful.
- There must be continuous involvement of all stakeholder groups in the ongoing implementation, review, evaluation, and correction of the plan.
- Measures must be clearly defined.
- There must be multiple measures of performance.
- The plan must be aligned with the district and school-level accountability goals.

Teachers have been found to be less resistant to pay-for-performance plans than may be assumed. Younger and new teachers are generally more supportive than their older and more experienced colleagues and less worried about favoritism and unhealthy competition and jealousy among teachers.[62]

However, pay for performance is an extremely complex technical and political endeavor, and even well-designed programs can fail if there are implementation glitches.

CASE EXAMPLE:

Denver Schools, Union Join Forces On Pay-for-Performance Pilot Effort

DENVER. The Denver Public Schools (DPS) and Denver Classroom Teachers Association (DCTA) collaborated in a pay-for-performance pilot program from 1999 until June 2003. In January 2004, the most significant of the systematic, longitudinal evaluations, conducted on the Denver plan, was released showing the results after four years.[63] After DCTA and the DPS worked together for four years to design the program, the union voted to pass it in March 2004.

Under the Denver Plan, teachers' compensation depends in part on measurable academic indicators including student growth, teacher knowledge and skills, and professional evaluation. Teachers who demonstrate success are rewarded with accelerated career earnings. Teachers who volunteer and are selected for difficult assignments, such as placements in special education positions or in failing schools, receive bonuses.

In devising the Denver Plan, DPS and DCTA agreed to collaborate in an experimental multi-year pilot program linking teacher compensation to measured student outcomes.

The parties negotiated the key elements of the pilot, which included:

- Creation of a four-member joint Design Team to design, oversee, implement, and evaluate the pilot;
- Limiting the initial scope of the pilot to a specific number of schools (12, initially);
- Allowing voluntary school participation, based on 85 percent of faculty votes;

- Establishing a Joint Task Force charged with designing and recommending for adoption a new teachers' compensation plan based in part on student achievement; and

- Commissioning a research study to evaluate the pilot.[64]

Joint Task Force Design objectives were not only meant to create a system that would reward teachers for high performance related directly to success in reaching specific instructional goals, but also to enhance the district's ability to attract and retain highly qualified teachers by other means. Accordingly, in addition to student growth, the Task Force also recommended that teacher

CONTRACT LANGUAGE EXAMPLES

2002-2005 Agreement and Partnership Between School District No. 1 in the City and County of Denver and The Denver Classroom Teachers Association. Appendix D.

The 2002-2005 collective-bargaining agreement between the Denver School District and the Denver Classroom Teachers Association includes an appendix entitled Pay for Performance Memorandum of Understanding. It contains eight sections, summarized as follows:

- **Commissioning of Design Team:** The team is responsible for planning, piloting, revising, implementing, and evaluating a performance pay plan.

- **Composition of Design Team:** There are two teachers and two administrators.

- **Responsibilities of Design Team:** The specific duties of the Design Team are listed, including implementation of a pilot program, training of participants and reporting on progress.

- **Assistance:** The design team is directed to use outside experts, and the Board and the Association agree to seek outside funding for the program.

- **Project Plan:** Required components of the performance pay plan are listed.

- **Participants and Elections:** The process for selection of schools that will participate in pay for performance is described.

- **Compensation:** Compensation of participating teachers is described.

- **Approval of Pay for Performance:** The Design Team is directed to issue a final report on the pay for performance by a date certain, after which the Board must approve a plan the Association will vote to accept or reject the plan.

Toledo Federation of Teachers and Toledo Public Schools. 2003. "Toledo Review and Alternative Compensations System (TRACS)." Introduction.

Toledo's "Plan for Alternative Compensation for Instructional Leadership" –TRACS—is described in detail in a booklet published by the Toledo Public School District and the Toledo Federation of Teachers in February 2003. The booklet contains the following introductory statement:

The 2001 contract negotiations between the Toledo Federation and the Toledo Board of Education focused on initiatives that have the potential to promote teacher quality and significantly improve the academic performance of urban youth. One of the initiatives that was mutually developed through these comprehensive discussions is the Toledo Review and Alternative Compensation System (TRACS). Both the union and the school district acknowledge that the traditional system of recognizing and compensating teachers might not lead to the type of student academic growth that is desired by the Board of Education, the Toledo Federation of Teachers, and the Toledo community. TRACS offers the opportunity to align enhanced compensation with exceptional teaching performance knowledge and skills, professional evaluation results, and market incentives qualify as bases for additional teacher pay.

In addition to offering voluntary participation, the Denver program offered important flexibility to schools opting to participate.

Accordingly, schools could choose from three different methods for measuring changes in student achievement under the program.

- **Approach One Schools** were those that chose to be evaluated on the basis of student progress as determined by a change in test scores on a norm-referenced student performance test (Iowa Test of Basic Skills).

- **Approach Two Schools** would be evaluated on the basis of student progress as determined by a change in test scores on a "criterion-referenced" test, or according to teacher-created measures.

- **Approach Three Schools** would be evaluated on the basis of teachers' acquisition of skills and knowledge.

Later in the project, the three different approaches were collapsed into one approach that involved both student learning outcome measures and professional development incentives.

Also, the 2003 Task Force proposal increased maximum teacher earnings potential from $65,000 for those with Ph.D.s and 25 years of service to $90,000, and made maximum earning attainable earlier in a teacher's career. The proposal also recommended that the district's previous policy of freezing cost-of-living adjustments for under-performing teachers be continued.[65]

While the Denver program provides teachers with substantial professional responsibility for improving student outcomes, it also offers teachers a professional and collaborative role in determining what specific outcomes should be, and how they should be assessed. For example, pilot school teachers set student learning objectives from year to year, either individually or as a team, and then seek building principal approval—instead of the reverse. At the end of the period, it is the teacher(s) who provide(s) evidence of achievement, based on data presented in a form previously agreed-upon. Accordingly, the process is objective and pre-determined. Also, individual student achievement is measured on the basis of progress over the course of an academic year, with success defined in terms of previously established goals that take into account individual student characteristics, such as socio-economic status. As a result, teachers are not disadvantaged by having difficult teaching assignments, nor are they discouraged from taking them.

The evaluation of the Denver pilot presents a complicated story.[66] There was a positive relationship between the goals teachers set for their students and the goals those students achieved. Over time, an increasing percentage of teachers raised their expected goals and attained them. Teachers with less than 15 years seniority did slightly better than those with more than 15 years (95 percent vs. 85 percent). Support for pay for performance grew among teachers in the pilot over time, as they became less fearful of the program's consequences.

However, achievement gains were not even. While middle and high school students in the pilot schools outperformed the students in the control schools, the same was not true for elementary school students—an unusual finding, running contrary to many evaluations, which report improvements to be less likely in middle and high schools than in elementary schools. In addition, the evaluation team cautioned that the pilot had challenged the district support systems and that areas of practice and policy must be strengthened when the pay-for-performance program goes to scale.

CASE EXAMPLE:

Toledo Initiative Places Educators On Different 'Tracs' to Improvement

TOLEDO, OHIO In 2001, the Toledo Federation of Teachers and the Toledo Public Schools jointly developed an initiative called the Toledo Review and Alternative Compensations System (TRACS). TRACS is a collaborative effort to improve teacher performance with voluntary and involuntary components.

TRACS is administered by a joint Professional Assignment and Compensation Committee (PAC), consisting of three teachers and two administrators. The teachers are appointed by the president of the union, and the administrators are appointed by the superintendent. Either the president or the superintendent can veto any proposed appointment. Leadership of the committee rotates from year to year between the district and the union.

TRACS includes three tracks, also called modules.

- **TRACS-A** is involuntary and designed to improve the performance of identified groups of teachers whose participation is required. Under TRACS-A the union and the district agree to materials and methods designed to address mutually identified performance deficits. Required content includes knowledge and skills training deemed necessary for improving student outputs, and individual performance evaluation to determine progress. Success or failure is determined by the school district's Staff Development and Control Board, consisting of teachers and administrators appointed by the president of the union and a designee of the superintendent.[67]
- **TRACS-B** is focused on school performance. It is designed to recognize and financially reward teachers in schools that meet or exceed previously determined high performance achievement goals. The improvement goals are established annually by PAC, and aligned with school-based improvement plans developed by individual school improvement committees. Schools can only participate in TRACS-B when the entire faculty agrees. Financial rewards are paid to individual faculty members.

- **TRACS-C** is focused on individual teacher performance. Participation is voluntary for every qualified teacher. Qualified teachers must have a minimum of five years successful teaching experience, at least three of which are in the Toledo schools. Qualification is determined by PAC, and is based on an evaluation of many factors, including evidence of continuous professional growth, peer respect, classroom excellence, writing proficiency, and good teaching strategies. TRACS-C has three levels: Career (1), Accomplished (2), and Distinguished (3). They represent a kind of career ladder. Each level involves specific requirements, duties, and functions and is subject to mandatory periodic evaluation. For example, Career Status (1) teachers must stay in the classroom, and select one specific area of student accountability to work on, and for which they are held accountable. Teachers may elect to stay at the Career (1) level, or apply for advancement to the Accomplished (2) level or the Distinguished (3) level. Accomplished (2) level teachers must also stay in the classroom, and may be assigned other duties such as peer evaluation, curriculum development, or others. Assignments are made by PAC. Distinguished (3) level teachers are also classroom teachers and may be assigned to difficult and high- needs areas for terms of not less than three years.

There are significant compensation incentives attached to all three levels in TRACS-C. Career Status (1) teachers receive an annual stipend equal to 5 percent of their base salary; Accomplished Status (2) teachers receive 10 percent and Distinguished Status (3) teachers receive 15 percent.

OTHER EXAMPLES OF DISTRICTS USING
PAY-FOR-PERFORMANCE PLANS

- Brevard County, Fla.
- Columbus, Ohio
- Douglas County, Colo.
- Memphis, Tenn.
- Nauset/Orleans, Mass.[68]
- Rochester, N.Y.

REFERENCES AND RESOURCES

- **Consortium for Policy Research in Education**
  Allan Odden, Co-Director
  University of Wisconsin-Madison
  1025 West Johnson Street, #653, Madison, WI 53706-1796
  Tel: 608.263.4260   Fax: 608.263.9390
  www.cpre.org
  arodden@wisc.edu

- **Community Training and Assistance Center**
  Source on Denver Plan
  30 Winter Street, Boston, MA 02108
  Tel: 617.423.1444   Fax: 617.423.4748
  ctac@ctacusa.com

- **Denver Public Schools**
  Andre Pettigrew, Assistant Superintendent
  for Administrative Services
  900 Grant Street, Denver, CO 80203
  Tel: 720.423.3271
  www.dpsk12.org

- **Toledo Federation of Teachers**
  Francine Lawrence, President
  111 S. Byrne Road, Toledo, OH 43615
  Tel: 419.535.3013   Fax: 419.535.0478
  www.tft250.org
  dallawrence@aol.com

- **Toledo Public Schools**
  Craig Cotner, Chief Academic Officer
  420 E. Manhattan Blvd., Toledo, OH 43608
  Tel: 419.729.8422
  www.tps.org
  craig.cotner@tps.org

CHAPTER FOOTNOTES

59. *The Toledo Plan*, Page 53.

60. 2001-2004 Agreement between the Toledo Federation of Teachers and the Toledo Public Schools. Article VXIII A-2.

61. See for example: Odden, A. and Kelley, C. (1997). *Paying teachers for what they know and do.* Corwin Press and Hassel, B.C. (2002). *Better pay for better teaching: Making teacher compensation pay off in the age of accountability.* Washington, D.C.: Progressive Policy Institute.

62. Public Agenda Foundation. (2003). *Stand by me: What teachers really think about unions, merit pay and other professional matters.* Washington, D.C.: Pp. 33-34.

63. William J. Slotnik, Maribeth D. Smith, Roberta J. Glass, and Barbara J. Helms. Community Training and Assistance Center (2004). *Catalyst for change: Pay for performance in Denver.* Boston. Available on the Internet at www.ctacusa.com/denver-vol3-final.pdf

64. William J. Slotnik, Maribeth D. Smith, Roberta J. Glass, and Barbara J. Helms. Community Training and Assistance Center (2004). *Catalyst for change: Pay for performance in Denver.* Boston. Available on the Internet at www.ctacusa.com/denver-vol3-final.pdf

65. Denver Public Schools-Denver Classroom Teachers Association Joint Task Force on Teacher Compensation draft, May 2003, *Compensation System for Teachers.*

66. William J. Slotnik, Maribeth D. Smith, Roberta J. Glass, and Barbara J. Helms. All results are from:

Community Training and Assistance Center (2004). *Catalyst for change: Pay for performance in Denver.* Boston. Available on the Internet at www.ctacusa.com/denver-vol3-final.pdf.

67. March 2, 2004, telephone interview with Dal Lawrence.

68. The 1999-2002 Nauset collective-bargaining agreement included a 1 percent incentive bonus if MCAS scores went up by stated amounts. The scores did go up, and the bonuses were paid. However, the language was not included in the successor contract.

EVALUATIONS BY FAMILIES AND SCHOOLS

Teachers send surveys to primary caregivers and/or students in order to solicit feedback about the usefulness of interactions between the home and school. Family members, including all primary caregivers, have a unique and important perspective on how well a teacher connects with their child. These caregivers also know how well the teacher is communicating with them, the adults whose support and cooperation are essential to the academic success of a child. Students, too, often have valuable insights because their reactions to their teachers can greatly influence their eagerness to learn. But formal teacher evaluation methods rarely include solicited input from families or students. When carefully gathered and responsibly interpreted, such data can be extremely useful in assessing teaching effectiveness, which in turn is essential to student achievement.

USEFULNESS TO IMPROVING STUDENT ACHIEVEMENT

The home-school connection is important to the learning of all students. Through these surveys, teachers receive feedback on which of their communication strategies best fit the needs and concerns of adult caregivers and students. Responses allow them to adjust their actions rather than wait until they receive complaints, unaware that different techniques would be helpful.

There are several reasons why some school districts have begun to survey families and students as part of the teacher evaluation process, including their unique vantage point as stakeholders outside of the bureaucracy and invested in the success of the system; and their ability to exercise choice both within and beyond a school district. Surveys provide systematic data collection, allow for comparisons over time, and enable evaluation about the engagement level of the parents, as well as their perception of the teacher.

Evaluation by parents raises concerns with some teachers who are wary of being judged by laypersons. Teachers worry that parents will use their own personal classroom experiences as guidelines for assessing them. Some parents may be experts in teaching and learning or have followed developments in the field; however, for most parents, pedagogical issues including content area and classroom management have changed drastically since they were students. As a result, evaluations by parents are typically limited to issues on which parents truly are expert. These issues may include feedback on the teacher's communication with parents and students; and/or the success of partnerships initiated by the teacher with the parent and child.

Teachers and union officers also worry that parent evaluations can be used by vocal parents to campaign against teachers who have offended or displeased them, no matter how legitimate the actions of the teacher. Surveys can, in fact, blunt

CONTRACT LANGUAGE EXAMPLES: EVALUATIONS BY FAMILIES AND SCHOOLS

July 1, 2002 Contractual Agreement Between The City School District of Rochester, New York and the Rochester Teachers Association. Section 52 (9).

Parent Surveys
The survey questions will be limited to home involvement and parent-teacher communications, and may address relevant aspects of a child's progress on which the committee is in Agreement that parents can effectively and appropriately comment....

... Parents completing the survey will be required to identify themselves on the form, and will remit the form to the appropriate teacher. The form will advise parents that they are encouraged to discuss any issue or concern directly with their child's teacher, will remind them of their existing right to contact a teacher's supervisor with relevant questions, concerns or positive comments, and, in this regard, will also inform parents that they may send a copy of the completed survey to a principal (or the appropriate administrator).

e. Completed surveys may be produced by the teacher during the annual review and the evaluator may similarly produce any forms which were copied to administration by parents.

Agreement Between The Minneapolis Federation of Teachers and Minneapolis Public Schools, 2203-2005. Article V, Section E.

Family and student feedback is an annual expectation for all educators. These surveys were developed with support from the City-wide Student Government; Research Evaluation and Assessment Departments, Planning and Policy and the Minneapolis Federation of Teachers. The family survey questions focus on home support, family involvement, family-teacher communications and student progress. Student surveys provide direct feedback to teachers on instruction, classroom environment and management, and relationships.

the effect of this sort of "witch hunt" by establishing norms across teachers in the same grade, reviewing parental feedback on the teacher from previous years, and in requiring explicit information about the type and frequency of parental interactions with the teacher.

CASE EXAMPLE:

District Plan Gives Parent Input Formal Role In Teacher Evaluation

ROCHESTER, N.Y. Soliciting feedback via a survey does not require that it be used for evaluative or disciplinary actions. Rochester, for example, refers to the survey as "an input form" not an "evaluation." Parent input into teacher evaluation was formalized in Rochester in 1998.[69] Using a Likert Scale (Usually, Sometimes, Rarely, Don't Know, or Doesn't Apply), the survey instrument first assesses the level of parental involvement in school activities by asking respondents how many different ways they have interacted with the school, including attending parent-teacher conferences, signing and returning report cards, visiting the school, and phoning or writing to the teacher. The remaining three sections of the one-page form ask parents to rate how frequently the teacher communicates with and involves them in the learning process, and how the teacher interacts with the child.

Feedback prompts include:

- The teacher responds clearly when I have questions about application of classroom rules to my child.
- The teacher deals with me in a fair and respectful manner.
- The teacher welcomes and considers information, which I provide in order to help my child.
- The teacher shares my high expectations for my child's learning and behavior.

CASE EXAMPLE:

District's Survey Questions Examine Home Supports, Family Involvement

MINNEAPOLIS. A multi-stakeholder group, including students, the district, and the teachers' union designed the survey instrument used in Minneapolis. The district translates family surveys into the district's five predominant languages. Survey questions focus on home support, family involvement, and family-teacher communications. The form advises the families that they are encouraged to discuss any issues directly with their child's teacher. Families will be informed that they may send a copy of the completed survey to the principal of the school. Family surveys are distributed on a fixed date; student surveys are conducted every marking period.

Student and family surveys are a formal part of the evaluation program for non-tenured teachers in Minneapolis and part of the annual evaluation of *all* teachers. The results of the completed student and family surveys may be used by the teacher for feedback and reflection with their Professional Development Process (PDP) team, and administrators may bring the feedback sent to them by parents to the PDP team.

OTHER EXAMPLES OF DISTRICTS WITH ASSESSMENTS BY FAMILIES AND SCHOOLS

- Department of Defense dependents' public schools
- District of Columbia Public Schools (Washington, D.C.)
- Wake County Public School System (Raleigh, N.C.)

RESOURCES AND REFERENCES

- **Minneapolis Federation of Teachers**
  Louise Sundin, President
  1300 Plymouth Avenue N., Minneapolis, MN 55411
  Tel: 612.529.9621   Fax: 612.529.0539
  www.MFT59.org

- **Minneapolis Public Schools**
  159 Pillsbury Drive SE, Minneapolis, MN 55455
  Tel: 612.625.7520   Fax: 612.624.8744
  kalni001@tc.umn.edu

- **Rochester Public Schools**
  Manuel J. Rivera, Superintendent
  131 West Broad Street, Rochester, NY 14614
  Tel: 585.262 8100
  www.rcsdk12.org
  manuel.rivera@rcsdk12.org

- **Rochester Teachers Association**
  Adam Urbanski, President
  30 N. Union Street, Suite 301, Rochester, NY 14607
  Tel: 585.546.2681
  www.rochesterteachers.com
  urbanski@rochesterteachers.com

CHAPTER FOOTNOTE

69. Koppich, J., Asher, K., Kerchner, C. (2003). *Developing careers, building a profession: The Rochester career in teaching plan.* Washington, D.C.: National Commission on Teaching & America's Future, Page 51.

CHAPTER 3

Devolving Centralized Control and Deregulating Schools

Devolution refers to the process whereby control and accountability for a public school system is decentralized from the central office downward to the school or outside the system to other entities.[1] Devolution is an international phenomenon in both developed and developing countries, especially those with national education systems.[2]

The organizational structure and control of public education has fluctuated over time to satisfy economic, political, and social conditions.[3] The Progressive reforms of the early 20th century centralized the locally controlled public schools, consolidating them into larger systems headed by professional experts accountable to the public through independent governance boards.[4] Public school systems, as well as other public and many private systems, adopted a managerial form known as "*bureaucratic centralism*" featuring strong centralized authority, vertical hierarchies of power, discretion, defined jobs in a

detailed division of labor, assumptions that expertise exists at the top of the hierarchy, rules and regulations governing behavior, and complex compliance regimes. These systems achieved the virtue of efficiency, largely through standardizing practice and economies of scale, strategies particularly effective in centralized systems.

Of course, in the century since the Progressive reforms there have been some notable fluctuations in the strict form of bureaucratic centralism largely as a response to political movements.[5] In 1969, New York City decentralized the public school system, establishing local school boards with hiring and budget authority. In 2003, the state legislature reversed course and abolished local control, putting the mayor in charge. Chicago and other urban school systems similarly have gone through several de- and re-centralization rounds. All systems fluctuate to some degree over time, and experiments over the degree of centralization and devolution are always occurring.

Centralized control was justified on the basis of efficiency. However, there is growing evidence that urban systems have grown so large that they exceed the point at which they benefit from economies of scale.[6] The conclusion of devolutionists is that standardized schooling is not working and neither is the organizational form that generates it:

"Reformers believe the source of problems is to be found in and around the schools, and that schools can be 'made' better by relying on existing institutions to impose the proper reforms... We believe existing institutions cannot solve the problem, because they are the problem—and that the key to better schools is institutional reforms."[7]

Today's devolution movement will likely have more staying power than earlier experiments. More than shifts in public tastes or experimentation by educational administrators are driving this change. Transformations in the organization of work, organizational structures, economic markets, and politics are occurring, all leading toward devolution. The scale and depth of these transformations are much like the ones in the early 1900s that brought on the centralized public school system model which lasted for 100 years.

The organization of knowledge work in both the public and private sector is changing. A greater portion of our economy is engaged in knowledge work, and a greater portion of each company and agency is doing knowledge work. In particular, technology-driven sectors of the economy are experimenting with organizational forms, authority relationships, and divisions of labor to find the best combinations for the generation and appropriation of new knowledge. These experiments are guided as much by new ideas about what constitutes knowledge and expertise, who generates it, the processes by which it is generated, and the way people and groups learn as they are by new information technologies.[8]

The organizational forms that are emerging from these changes are marked by lateral communication rather than orders emanating from the top of the organization. The role of the leader is being transformed from director and monitor to catalyst for learning and action. Implementation bubbles from the bottom where the work is done, upward through the organization. The members of the organization engage in dialogue and participate in every aspect of the work. The organization reacts to the customer or student who enters, adapting to them rather than forcing the customer to adapt to the organization. The organization "learns" from its interactions with customers and students, and that knowledge is shared across levels and functions of the organization.

Translating this abstraction into concrete terms: imagine a school that makes few assumptions about a student and has few standard operating procedures and routines. All members of the staff engage with and learn about the student and tailor the educational environment so that it meets the needs of the student. They constantly monitor the usefulness of their adaptations to the student and share what they have learned with other practitioners.

Changes in economic forms are also driving devolution. Rather than the efficiency-based mass production for mass markets paradigm that characterized manufacturing and service industries in the 20th century, economic entities are specializing, catering only to niche markets, foregoing customers who do not fit their niche profile or who are too expensive to service. These organizations create their profits not from efficiencies and volume but by offering choice, service, and identity branding. Consumers are bringing the experience of private sector niche marketing and the expectations for customization and service to the public school system and find the system lacking.

At the same time, a political movement has grown over the past 20 years that challenges the definitions of government that were forged during the New Deal and in the Cold War era. The logic and language of market transactions is used to shape and describe political choices. Education in this philosophy is a private good, not a universal public good. Families, not society, are the important stakeholders. This movement, steeped in libertarian philosophy and rational choice economics, argues for limited government regulation, limited taxes, and fewer public goods and services rather than efficient government. Government is seen as a monopoly provider that needs competition from alternative providers.

A *"new managerialism"* has emerged in

the public sector focused on "steering, not rowing."[9] Public managers contract with and monitor service providers rather than oversee production or delivery of services.[10] Support is growing for "choice" rather than the collective provision of public goods and services.[11] Public organizations such as public school systems are decentralizing and specializing.[12] Functions such as budgeting and personnel are pushed to the site level. Organizations are held accountable through performance measures rather than through bureaucratic means. The people working in them are motivated by professional standards and rewarded for differential levels of performance.

The three innovations described in Chapter Three—site-based management, high-autonomy schools, and small learning communities—represent ways that decentralization is changing public education.

SITE-BASED MANAGEMENT AND ACCOUNTABILITY

Site-based management shifts decision-making power and governance downward from the district central office to the school level. Decisions about many issues, sometimes including budget allocation and spending, personnel, curriculum, and the school day, are now made at the school level rather than at the district level. Many schools have a school site council whose members may include teachers, parents, and community members.

USEFULNESS TO IMPROVING STUDENT ACHIEVEMENT

Research conducted in several districts has shown that student achievement appears to improve in schools using site-based management.[13] One-size-fits-all decisions made at central levels may inappropriately address the conditions, needs, or preferences of a given school and its community. Site-based management allows decision-making to occur closer to the learning environment. As a result, decisions can be tailored to the unique circumstances of a school site, students, and the community. Teachers, parents, and community members can assume new leadership roles through site-based management. Participation in decision-making recognizes the professionalism of teachers and allows them to exercise leadership.

More than half of all states have legislation promoting or authorizing site-based management.[14] Schools practicing site-based management must still adhere to general performance standards established centrally. However, under site-based-management-specific strategies, programs and plans for meeting those standards are determined by schools or other small learning units. Program and school site staff members are able to develop academic and operational strategies—based on their particularized insights, knowledge, and experience—to support student success in their own small settings.

Much of the research done on site-based management has cautioned that, to be successful, it entails both structurally decentralizing decision-making at a school level, and implementing participatory decision-making by stakeholders. Weak implementation of either component threatens to diminish the success of site-based management. Concern has been raised that the actual decentralization of decision-making is often not as smooth and comprehensive as intended. For example, complications may occur if school budgeting cannot be meaningfully separated from district budgeting. Additionally, without the second component—participatory decision-making by stakeholders—the innovation is incomplete and unlikely to yield improvements in student achievement.[15]

In most site-based management and accountability models, the school board develops performance goals for the district, and schools establish committees (that include teachers and administrators), which operate as site-based governing bodies.

The roles and authority of the governing bodies vary, in some cases encompassing the determination of:

- Instructional methods consistent with the board's stated goals and objectives
- Student grouping and scheduling
- Student disciplinary procedures
- Teacher hiring
- Evaluation and training
- Budget development and oversight

Site-based management models also vary in significant ways. In some districts, participation in site-based management is voluntary, on a school-by-school basis.[16] Some site-based management systems enable formal input by parents and/or students.[17] Some are required to adopt bylaws approved by parents and teachers, and some facilitate site-base flexibility by permitting temporary waivers to existing provisions of master contracts when approved by a majority of union members.[18]

CASE EXAMPLE:

District, Union Team Up For School-Based Planning

ROCHESTER, N.Y. Beginning in 1991-1992, the Rochester Teachers Association (RTA) and the Rochester Board of Education agreed to "cooperatively participate in the development of school based planning at each school location."[19] Since that time, schools have been involved in the development of strategies, terms, and performance goals for which they are held individually accountable. Each school (or smaller learning unit) negotiates a binding, multi-year plan for improvement. Plans are based on school-specific data, including student performance, student mobility, and teacher absenteeism, among other things. Plans include sections on needs assessment, goals, strategies, and monitoring and

CONTRACT LANGUAGE EXAMPLES

2003-2005 Agreement Between The Minneapolis Board of Education and The Minneapolis Federation of Teachers. Preamble.

The Importance of School-Based Decision-Making. We believe that decision making is best closest to and including the students being served. Each school community has the best information and position to craft appropriate and effective strategies for the task at hand, with the primary task being the continuous improvement of student achievement. The school is where people make a difference in the daily life of each student. School-based decision making brings these people together who then share the responsibility for needed changes and the corresponding accountability for results achieved.

evaluation processes. Negotiated improvement goals become targets for annual progress. Schools that demonstrate improvement in student performance and overall effectiveness earn greater autonomy, flexibility, and discretion in the use of resources. Schools that do not improve become candidates for intervention by teams, consisting of teachers, administrators, parents, and (in high schools) even students.

CASE EXAMPLE:

Minneapolis Contract Emphasizes Importance of Site Leadership Teams

MINNEAPOLIS. In the current contract between the Minneapolis Federation of Teachers and the Minneapolis School Board, parties state their belief that each school community has the best information and is in the best position to craft appropriate and effective strategies for the tasks at hand, with the primary task being the continuous improvement of student achievement. The parties commit to school-based decision-making and school-based accountability for results.

The contract calls for site leadership teams in each school. Team members are appointed and elected. They represent all major stakeholders in the schools, including staff, family, community members, and students. Staff is defined to include the school principal, union steward, elected teachers in the school, and other employees.

Site leadership teams operate in accordance with bylaws that they adopt. Bylaws for different sites may vary, but they must address specified governance issues, such as team member terms, protocols for the solicitation of ideas from outside the team, and specified methods for communicating team decisions. Numerous site

---

2000-2003 Agreement Between The Board of Education of the City School District of The City of New York and United Federation of Teachers. Article 8A.

The Union and the Board agree that SBM/SDM is a process in which all members of the school committee collaborate in identifying issues, defining goals, formulating policy and implementing programs. The uniqueness of each school community requires that the SBM/SDM process and the organizational and instructional issues discussed are determined by the staff, parents, administrators and students (where appropriate) at individual schools through the SBM/SDM team. The union and the Board agree that in order to achieve SBM/SDM at the school level significant restructuring of instruction must occur, and the parties agree to work cooperatively in an effort to bring about these changes.

2003-2005 Agreement between Eugene Education Association and Eugene School District 4J. Article 18.8.

SAFETY NET CLAUSE: The parties recognize that our mutual exploration of SBDM may result in unforeseen difficulties or problem areas. Since our initial foray into SBDM is largely experimental, we agree that either party may want to slow down or halt, at least temporarily, the movement toward SBDM. The safety net is established for this purpose. To initiate the safety net process, the Association or District must send the other a letter stating the concerns and reasons for instituting the safety net. The parties shall then have 30 days to resolve the initiating parties' concerns. If the concerns are not resolved after thirty 30) days, then all plans for extending approval for the additional sites to SBDM shall be placed on "hold" until the parties reach an agreement on how to proceed. The parties agree to use a mutually acceptable facilitator to bring resolution.

team responsibilities are stated in the contract, and their scope is comprehensive.

Responsibilities include:

- Management and operation of the school
- Budget development and oversight
- Development and implementation of a School Improvement Plan
- Regular communication with staff and community
- School staffing
- Leadership transition plans when necessary
- Promotion of a professional climate
- Participation in professional development, and more

CASE EXAMPLE:

Agreement Promotes Uniqueness Of Every School Community

NEW YORK, N.Y. The United Federation of Teachers (UFT) and the Board of Education in New York City have negotiated a process they call SBM/SDM—school-based management/shared decision-making. Introductory contract language states a joint belief that the uniqueness of each school community requires organizational and instructional issues to be determined at the school level by staff, parents, administration, and (at the high schools) students. The parties agree to work cooperatively to achieve SBM/SDM.[20]

Participation in the SBM/SDM program is voluntary and determined on a school-by-school basis based upon the agreement of the principal and superintendent and on the vote of non-supervisory staff. Prior to 2002, 75 percent approval was required; in 2002 the required percentage dropped to 55 percent. Schools signing up for the program can drop out when 55 percent of the voting non-supervisory staff so choose.

Schools participating in SBM/SDM select local management teams. Aside from the stipulation that the school UFT chapter leader must be a member, each school can determine the composition of its management team. Each management team determines the range of issues it will address and the decision-making process it will use.[21]

CASE EXAMPLE:

Eugene Plan Includes 'Safety Net Clause'

EUGENE, ORE. The 2003-2004 agreement between the Eugene Education Association and Eugene School District 4J contains extensive language on site-based decision-making. The parties state their belief that site-based decision-making has the potential to improve education, foster mutual respect, provide greater employee empowerment, improve the quality and extent of parent involvement, create an environment which is more responsible (sic) to the client needs and concerns, and encourage the collegial exchange of ideas. Accordingly, the parties pledge themselves to give site-based management a try—they commit "to an honest and mutual examination and trial of site-based decision making."[22]

What follows are sections establishing a joint steering committee and other conditions, including that site participation shall be strictly voluntary; that the district shall fund training, compensation, and implementation from sources other than staffing; and that specific contract waivers may be recommended by the Steering Committee. Perhaps most significant is the "Safety Net Clause," which allows either party to "slow down or halt, at least temporarily" the site-based management process.[23]

ADDITIONAL DISTRICTS THAT HAVE USED
SITE-BASED MANAGEMENT

- Bellevue, Wash.
- Boston
- Chicago
- Dade County, Fla.
- Hammond, Ind.
- Seattle
- Toledo, Ohio

REFERENCES AND RESOURCES

- **Cornell University**
  Edward E. Lawler, III, Professor
  Industrial and Labor Relations & Sociology
  309 Ives Hall Cornell University, Ithaca, NY 14853
  Tel: 607.255.2185   Fax: 607.255.7774
  ejl@cornell.edu

- **Minneapolis Public Schools**
  Patricia Thornton, Coordinator
  College-School Collaborations in Teacher Development
  159 Pillsbury Drive SE , Minneapolis, MN 55455
  Tel: 612.625.8974   Fax: 612.624.8744
  kalni001@tc.umn.edu

- **Minneapolis Federation of Teachers**
  Louise Sundin, President
  67 8th Avenue, NE, Minneapolis, MN 55413
  Tel: 612.529.9621   Fax: 612.529.0539
  www.MFT59.org
  lsundin@mft59.org

- **New York City**
  United Federation of Teachers (UFT)
  Lucille Swaim, Coordinator of Negotiations
  52 Broadway Avenue, New York, NY 10004
  Tel: 212.777.7500
  www.uft.org

- **New York City Department of Education**
  Joel I. Klein, Chancellor
  Chancellor's Office
  52 Chamber Street, New York, NY 10007
  Tel: 718.935.2000
  www.nycenet.edu

- **Rochester Public Schools**
  Manuel J. Rivera, Superintendent
  131 West Broad Street, Rochester, NY 14614
  Tel: 585.262 8100
  www.rcsdk12.org
  manuel.rivera@rcsdk12.org

- **Rochester Teachers Association**
  Adam Urbanski, President
  30 N. Union Street, Suite 301, Rochester, NY 14607
  Tel: 585.546.2681
  www.rochesterteachers.com
  urbanski@rochesterteachers.com

- **Eugene School District 4J**
  George Russell, Superintendent
  200 North Monroe Street, Eugene, OR 97402
  Tel: 541.687.3123
  russell_g@4j.lane.edu

- **Eugene Education Association**
  Paul Duchin, President
  200 North Monroe Street, Eugene, OR 97402
  Tel: 541.687.3321

CHAPTER FOOTNOTES

1. This chapter will only address decentralization and devolution from the center of the public school system downward to schools. There are more radical forms of devolution occurring in public education, including contract schools, Internet-based programs, and home schooling, that will not be addressed here.

2. See Geoff Whitty, Sally Power, and David Halpin. 1998. *Devolution and Choice in Education: The School, the State and the Market.* Philadelphia: Open University Press; Allison Bullock and Hywel Thomas. 1997. *Schools at the Centre? A Study of Decentralisation.* London: Rutledge. The World Bank has a variety of studies and reports on this phenomenon as well. See www.worldbank.org

3. Richard W. Scott. 1992. *Organizations: Rational, Natural and Open Systems.* 3rd ed. New York: Prentice-Hall.

4. See Raymond E. Callahan. 1962. *Education and the Cult of Efficiency.* Chicago: University of Chicago Press; David B. Tyack. 1974. *The One Best System: A History of American Urban Education.* Cambridge, Mass.: Harvard University Press.

5. David Tyack. "School Governance in the United States: Historical Puzzles and Anomalies." In Jane Hannaway, Martin Carnoy, (eds.) 1993. *Decentralization and School Improvement.* San Francisco: Jossey-Bass.

6. Research on the negative benefits of size can be found in Gerry E. Hendershot and Thomas F. James. "Size and Growth as Determinants of Administrative-Production Rations in Organizations." *American Sociological Review. Volume 37* (April 1972) and John Kasarda. "The Structural Implications of Social System Size. *American Sociological Review.* Volume 39 (February 1974), among others.

7. John E. Chubb and Terry M. Moe. 1990. *Politics, Markets and America's Schools.* Washington, D.C.: Brookings Institution.

8. Some of these ideas come from chaos and complexity theory, and include the "self organizing system," best reflected in Peter Senge, 1990. *Fifth Discipline: The Art and Practice of the Learning Organization.* New York: Doubleday. Advances in cognitive science have helped to explain the "distributed theories of the mind," from which the notion of "distributed leadership emerges, in part." See Tomas Hellstrom, Ulf Malmquist, and Jo Mikaelssone. "Decentralizing Knowledge: Managing Knowledge Work in a Software Engineering Firm." *Journal of High Technology Management Research.* Volume 2 (3).

9. David Osborne and Ted Gaebler, 1992. *Reinventing Government: How the Entrepreneurial Spirit is Transforming the Public Sector.* Reading, Mass.: Addison-Wesley.

10. Paul T. Hill. 1997. "Contracting in Public Education." In Diane Ravitch and Joseph P. Viteritti (eds.) *New Schools for a New Century: The Redesign of Urban Education.* New Haven: Yale University Press.

11. While vouchers are beyond the scope of this work, it must be mentioned that they represent the organizational form preferred by devolutionists.

12. Pat O'Brien and Barry Down. 2002. "What are Teachers Saying about New Managerialism?" *Journal of Education Enquiry.* Volume 3. No. 1.

13. Hess, G.A. (1999). Expectation, opportunity, capacity and will: The essential components of Chicago School Reform. *Educational Policy.* 13,3, Pp. 494-517.

14. For example, in Massachusetts, state law establishes school councils. These councils are involved in recommendations, including on the school budget. See Chapter 71. 59c (7).

15. Bimber, B. (1993.) *School decentralization: Lessons from the study of bureaucracy.* Santa Monica: RAND. Page 36. Also see Weiss, S. (2001). School-based management: Rhetoric vs. reality. *The Progress of Education Reform: 1999-2001.* Denver: Education Commission of the States; Wohlstetter, P. and Mohrman, S.A.. (1993). School-based management strategies for success. *CPRE Finance Briefs.* Philadelphia: Consortium for Policy Research in Education.

16. Cincinnati is an example.

17. New York City is an example.

18. Boston and Minneapolis adopt bylaws. Boston and New York City use waivers.

19. Agreement between the City School District of Rochester, N.Y., and the Rochester Teachers Association. July 1, 2002. Section 54.

20. 2002-2003 Agreement between the New York City Board of Education and the United Federation of Teachers. Article Eight, A.

21. Ibid.

22. Article 23

23. ii Section 18.8

HIGH-AUTONOMY SCHOOLS

High-autonomy schools are "in-district" charter schools that operate with even more freedom and flexibility than schools with site-based management. These schools are often released from many district regulations and have flexibility with regard to their mission, governance, budgeting, management, union regulations, and accountability requirements. In contrast to conventional charter schools, which are enabled by state statute, high-autonomy schools are established at the district-level through district-specific agreements between the administration, school board, and teachers' union. In some cases, teachers and teachers' unions are engaged in the conversion of traditional schools into high-autonomy schools. In other instances, an education management company or a parent/community group is involved in their management. High-autonomy schools are typically smaller than traditional public schools, specialized in their curriculum, and have routines and regulations established at the school level. High-autonomy schools are attractive to many parents because they offer a choice of schools, specialized curricula, and pedagogical focus. Similarly, many educators elect to work in high-autonomy schools, where teacher ownership, flexible work arrangements, and increased site-based control result in a challenging and rewarding professional environment.

USEFULNESS TO IMPROVING STUDENT ACHIEVEMENT

Evidence is lacking on the effects of high-autonomy schools on student achievement, particularly among poor and minority children. However, high-autonomy schools are generally established with the goal of providing a more responsive learning environment for students, in which specific student and community needs can be addressed in the school's design and management. These schools offer public school options to parents who cannot change their residence. Additionally, they provide competition to what some call "monopoly" public schools. Given the increasing popularity of this model among families, students, and educators, the prevalence of high-autonomy schools will likely grow.

Across the nation, districts are electing to establish high-autonomy schools to better serve students and create increasingly satisfying and challenging professional opportunities for educators. The case example discussed in this section provides information pertaining to Boston's experience with pilot schools, but this trend has taken root in many other regions. Rochester, N.Y., and Milwaukee have both experimented extensively with high-autonomy schools and demonstrate alternative strategies for the implementation of this type of innovative practice. The principle of site-based management, explained in the previous section, is central in high-autonomy schools. The difference is that high-autonomy schools are formally designated as distinct from other schools in the district and are afforded a level of independence that does not extend to most other schools.

CASE EXAMPLE:

Pilot Schools Represent District's 'Research and Development' Arm

BOSTON. Boston pilot schools represent an innovative model of reform, featuring deregulation and the opportunity for program customization in whole-school settings. In contrast with charter schools, which were authorized under the *Massachusetts Education Reform* Act of 1993, Boston's pilot schools were established through a district-level agreement between Boston's district, union, and political leadership. Pilot schools have some of the characteristics of both small learning communities and site-based management models. The Boston school district describes pilot schools as its "research and development arm," intended to develop best practices and serve as a catalyst for change.[24]

In 1994, the mayor of Boston, Boston Public Schools (BPS), and Boston Teachers Union (BTU) jointly established the Boston pilot schools. The purpose of these schools was the promotion of education reform and improvement of student outcomes in experimental settings where individual school autonomy is increased. Most significantly, the pilot schools were exempted from union work rules that apply to other schools throughout the district.[25] In addition, pilot schools were created to "promote increased choice options within the school district, largely in response to 1993 state legislation creating first-time charter schools and the subsequent loss of Boston students to area charter schools."[26] Together, the Mayor's Office, BPS, and the BTU requested and evaluated proposals submitted by existing schools looking to convert. There were 19 pilot schools in Boston serving approximately 5,700 students during the 2003-2004 school year.[27]

The pilot school vision is centered on improving student outcomes through the creation of small, flexible learning communities of teachers and students that are focused on a rigorous curriculum.

Some guiding principles include:

- **Leadership development** through democratic processes including administrators, teachers, students, and parents;
- **Shared accountability** work within and among pilot schools to recognize and develop the best systems; and
- **Political advocacy** and active promotion of successful policies and community organizing to engage more constituencies in pilot school reform efforts.[28]

Teachers at pilot schools remain members of the bargaining unit. Pilot school teachers retain seniority and are guaranteed, at a minimum, contract salary and benefits. However, teachers in the pilot schools are required to abide by the terms of an individual pilot school plan, as well. Such terms may include special requirements involving the length of the school day and year, the amount of time required beyond the regular day,

CONTRACT LANGUAGE EXAMPLE

2003-2006 Collective Bargaining Agreement between the Boston Teachers Union and the Boston School Committee. Article III, Section D.

The Boston Public Schools and the Boston Teachers Union are sponsoring the establishment of innovative pilot schools within the Boston Public School system. The purpose of establishing pilot schools is to provide models of educational excellence that will help to foster widespread educational reform throughout all Boston Public Schools. The parties hope to improve dramatically the educational learning environment and thereby improve student performance...

Employees in the Pilot Schools will be required to work the full work day/work year as prescribed by the terms of the individual pilot school proposal. Nothing in this Agreement shall prevent Pilot School governing bodies from making changes to their programs and schedules during the year.

1994 Boston Teachers Union Contract.

"Pilot Schools will operate with an average school-based per pupil budget, plus a start-up supplement, and will have greatly increased decision-making authority, including exemptions from all Union and School Committee work rules...Employees in Pilot schools will be required to work the full work day/work year as prescribed by the terms of the individual Pilot school proposal. Further, they shall be required to perform and work in accordance with the terms of the individual Pilot school proposal."

additional time required during the summer or school vacations, and assignment of duties beyond the negotiated contract.

Only teachers who volunteer are assigned to pilot schools. In volunteering, teachers agree to the special set of policies, rules, and working conditions that are prescribed by the individual pilot school plans. Each pilot school develops an internal appeals process that is managed by a joint union/district committee and enables any staff member to raise issues.[29]

The autonomy of the Boston pilot schools extends to nearly every area of operation, including staffing, the budget, curriculum and assessment, governance and policies, and the calendar.

Highlights of pilot schools autonomy include:

- **Staffing**. Pilot schools are able to hire from and fire their own staff into an unassigned employee pool. This flexibility is intended to facilitate the creation of a cohesive staff that matches each school's unique student populations, goals, and cultures.

- **Budget.** Pilot schools receive an initial start-up sum from the district and thereafter they are funded according to the same formulas as non-pilot schools at the same grade levels. In contrast to traditional schools operating with the Boston Public Schools, pilot schools have total discretion with respect to spending. Additionally, in some areas they are able to choose whether to purchase direct central-office services from the district.

- **Curriculum and Assignment.** While pilot schools must comply with all district and state standardized testing requirements, they are freed from local district curriculum requirements. Thus, they may choose to develop school-based curricula and any additional assessment practices.

- **Governance and Policies.** Pilot schools need not adhere to most district governance policies, but instead can create their own. For example, pilot schools can exert control over budget approval processes, the selection and retention of the principal, and the creation and modification or termination of school programs.

- **Calendar.** Pilot schools are not bound by the district's calendar and have the flexibility to lengthen the school day and/or school year. Pilot schools can also reorganize their use of time to allow for special programs and activities, such as time for teachers to work together without students.[30]

Boston pilot schools have recently been evaluated on their efficacy.[31] Enrolling a population that is "generally representative" of Boston Public Schools, the pilot schools score favorably both on "climate" and academic achievement. These schools have better attendance, longer waiting lists for entry, less mobility among students (signaling a greater "holding power"), and fewer suspensions than conventional public schools in Boston. Even more impressive is the performance of students in pilot schools on the state assessment examinations. Ten of the 13 elementary schools score comparably or better than conventional schools on English, Language Arts, and Mathematics. The pilot high school scores above all non-examination high schools. Four of five pilot middle schools are among the higher performers in the district.

ADDITIONAL DISTRICTS THAT HAVE IMPLEMENTED HIGH-AUTONOMY SCHOOLS

- Dade County, Fla.

- Milwaukee

- New York, N.Y.

- Rochester, N.Y.

REFERENCES AND RESOURCES

- **Boston Teachers Union**
  Richard Stutman, President
  180 Mt. Vernon Street, Boston, MA 02125
  Tel: 617.BTU.2000
  www.btu.org
  rstutman@btu.org

- **Boston Public Schools**
  Thomas W. Payzant, Superintendent
  26 Court Street, 7th floor, Boston, MA 02108
  Tel: 617.635.9050
  Fax: 617.635.9059
  www.boston.k12.ma.us

CHAPTER FOOTNOTES

24. The Boston Pilot Schools Network Vision Statement. www.ccebos.org/pilotschools/bostonpilotschools.htm

25. The 2001-2003 agreement states that pilot schools are not allowed to waive contract provisions with respect to salary, benefits, or layoff procedures.

26. The Boston Pilot Schools Network History and Purpose. http://www.ccebos.org/pilotschools/

history.html Checked on Jan. 18, 2004.

27. Approximately 9 percent of students in the Boston Public School District attended pilot schools in 2003-2004.

28. The Boston Pilot Schools Network Vision Statement. www.ccebos.org/pilotschools/bostonpilotschools.htm

29. Much in the information in this section is taken from the 2000-2003 collective-bargaining agreement between the Boston Teacher Union and

the Boston School Committee.

30. Boston Pilot School Network Web site. www.ccebos.org/pilotschools/conditions.html. Accessed Jan. 8, 2004.

31. Tung, Rosann, Monique Ouimette, and Jay Feldman. "How are Boston Pilot School Students Faring? Student Demographics Engagement and Performance 1998-2003." Presented at American Educational Research Association. San Diego. March 2004. Center for Collaborative Education. Boston.

SMALL LEARNING COMMUNITIES

Small learning communities provide alternatives to large, comprehensive schools, particularly secondary schools. They exist as: 1) stand-alone schools that are restructured from existing schools; 2) newly established schools; or 3) "school-within-a-school" academies that are co-located within a larger school. The theory behind small learning communities is that reform efforts should be focused on "the smallest feasible unit of organized learning, i.e., the schools."[32]

USEFULNESS TO IMPROVING STUDENT ACHIEVEMENT

Small learning communities address the contradiction that exists between learning and teaching (intensely interactive human processes) and large institutions (impersonal, routinized, and inflexible structures). Individual schools can be more responsive to student needs than whole school districts, and small schools are more adaptive than large ones. The premise is that students in small settings get more attention, are less apt to get lost, can develop a sense of belonging, and are held more accountable.[33] Research is beginning to document the effects of small learning communities on student outcomes, extending beyond test score gains to examine reduction in drop-out rates and discipline problems.

Public schools, particularly high schools, have grown very large over the past century—doubling in average size over the past generation. Two factors have influenced this trend. The first is the belief that fewer, but larger schools are more cost effective than more numerous, but smaller schools. The second is the development of the comprehensive school, which offers a wide range of grades, courses, programs, and services. Some high schools have grown so large that they resemble community college campuses. Other high schools have so many students, attending on staggered schedules, that they are larger than small towns. In rural areas, the regional high schools are often long distances from students' homes, thus necessitating hours of travel and separating students from teachers and friends.

Large, impersonal institutions have a powerful effect on the nature of human interactions. In large schools, teachers may work with up to 150 students over the course of a day. Interactions are brief and impersonal, by necessity. Class offering are wide, but there may be no coherence across the curriculum. Distraction results from noise levels and frenetic activity created by masses of people, eating, moving through corridors, and even engaging in play or learning. Students move through a daily course schedule, often not seeing the same learners more than once. Anonymity fosters more anomie and with it, more anti-social behavior.[34]

None of these conditions are conducive to enabling focus, personalized attention, or finding one's own voice. Nor are large schools likely to provide social and emotional development, which are foundational supports for academic success. The school experience *could* be a stabilizing influence for children at risk; however, it is little wonder that large, impersonal schools are not meeting the needs of many poor, minority, and otherwise stressed adolescents.

Small learning communities are characterized by their attempt to personalize the learning experience. In the best designs, small learning communities offer less bureaucracy and, frequently, opportunities to customize programs. They often have some independent authority to develop curriculum, policy, and culture specific to their populations and settings.

Schools that become small learning communities often adopt a site-based decision-making structure, as well—illustrating the inter-relatedness of these concepts. Many pilot schools in Boston, for example, are organized as small learning communities with site-based decision-making.

Support for small learning communities comes from policymakers, foundation sponsors,[35] and the public.[36] The federal government has a competitive grant program designed to assist schools (enrolling at least 1,000 students and offering grades 11 and 12) develop and implement strategies for creating small learning communities. These funds can be used for teacher professional development and include a wide range of stakeholders: parents, the business community, and community-based organizations.[37]

However, research shows that "size is not a panacea" in and of itself.[38] According to a Public Agenda survey, teachers described fewer differences between large and small high schools. A different, qualitative study comparing a large and small high school showed that, though relationships were more positive, some students felt they benefited from anonymity, particularly if they felt their family background was a stigma.[39]

Restructuring existing schools is very difficult and may take a longer time to show differences in practice and outcomes than new small learning communities.[40] Both strategies can achieve smaller size, but not necessarily impact the learning atmosphere. Various types of small learning communities experience ranging levels of success.

However, when implemented deftly, small size can offer "three R's: rigorous instruction, relevant curriculum and supportive relationships."[41] These conditions allow learning communities to develop an organizational culture marked by the way teachers can interact with students, with each other, and with administrators.[42] As a result, teachers and administrators work more frequently in cross-disciplinary and cross-functional teams. This collaboration results in several things. School routines and practices become more student-centered. Schedules and learning designs can be more flexible. Teachers can delve deeper in content areas. There is more collegial support for high-quality teaching, and discipline becomes more manageable.

There is some evidence that smaller learning communities are more economically efficient than earlier assumed, especially if both the benefits and costs are weighed. While per-student costs may appear higher, the average graduation rate at smaller schools is considerably higher, so the cost per graduate may be lower.[43] Smaller learning communities also benefit from cost savings because they have smaller administrative staffing requirements and experience less vandalism and other forms of destruction.[44]

Evidence of the effects of smaller learning communities on student achievement is starting to emerge.[45] A study of small schools in four states showed a narrowing achievement gap between poor students and more affluent students on state assessment tests.[46] A five-year study of five small learning communities created out of a single comprehensive high school in New York City showed similar findings. Despite the fact that the students in these communities were less affluent, more linguistically diverse, and lower achieving than students in the control school, they scored higher on reading and writing and comparably on math tests.[47] While the graduation rate for New York City schools is 70 percent of students graduating within seven years, 84.6 percent of students in the smaller learning communities graduated within six years.

The goal of small learning communities is to develop a nurturing atmosphere where students know one another and their teachers. Often small learning communities have different subject specialties and approaches to learning and school environments. Many small learning communities incorporate advisor or mentoring systems, so that every student is paired with an adult in the building, and every teacher has a small group of students for which he or she is particularly responsible.[48]

CASE EXAMPLE:

Cluster Strategies Look To Build Personal Sense in Big High Schools

SOMERVILLE, MASS., AND FENWAY HIGH SCHOOL, BOSTON. In Somerville, a large high school has created a house structure for ninth and 10th graders to create a sense of personalization and break down the large-group atmosphere. Students are organized into small learning groups, or clusters, each sized at approximately 100 students. Clustered groups attend classes together and have the same teachers throughout the school day.[49] A similar system is in place at the Fenway High School in Boston.[50] Students stay in the same small groups during the day and have the same teachers from year to year. Students and teachers all get to know each other and tend to act as a community within the larger setting.[51]

CONTRACT LANGUAGE EXAMPLES

2.26.03 Side letter on Small Learning Communities between the Worcester School Committee and the Education Association of Worcester.

Side Letter, Small Learning Communities
As the parties are aware, the School District Leadership Team has been working, and continues to work, on the creation of small learning communities at the secondary level as part of the Carnegie efforts in the District…

It is the consensus of all parties that for these small learning communities to be successful, the Committee and the Association must work collaboratively and in the best interests of the students of these schools…

With all of this in mind the parties will agree to utilize this side letter and the agreements contained herein to accomplish the flexibilities required to make the small learning communities successful without making permanent modifications to the underlying collective bargaining agreement. The parties are in agreement that this side letter shall not authorize modifications in the following areas of the contract: Grievance Procedure; Leaves of Absence with or without pay; Sick Leave; Supervision and Evaluation; Transfers; Reduction in Force; and Dismissal of Teachers. Any area of governance will not be included in this side letter…

CASE EXAMPLE:

Carnegie Grant Helps Worcester Build Smaller Learning Environments

WORCESTER, MASS. Worcester is one of seven school districts in the nation to have received a substantial multi-year grant from the Carnegie Foundation to restructure middle and high schools to improve student outcomes.[52] A major initiative of the grant is to create smaller learning environments. In Worcester, the goal is to develop both small schools and small learning communities within existing schools. Worcester's small schools and small learning communities are intended to have different specialty areas, learning methods, and community cultures. Both the teachers and the district have recognized that such differentiations may require adjustments to the existing contract, and that every small learning unit may well have special needs. To address the situation, the Worcester School Committee and the Educational Association of Worcester have entered into a side letter that authorizes the parties to consider changes to the master agreement.[53]

A side letter has been developed, and formal plans have been drawn at each of the schools where small learning communities are contemplated.

OTHER DISTRICTS WITH SMALL LEARNING COMMUNITIES

- Boston

- Los Angeles

- New York, N.Y.

- Providence, R.I.

- Toledo, Ohio

REFERENCES AND RESOURCES

- **Boston Public Schools**
  Thomas W. Payzant, Superintendent
  26 Court Street, 7th floor, Boston, MA 02108
  Tel: 617.635.9050   Fax: 617.635.9059
  www.boston.k12.ma.us

- **Boston Teachers Union**
  Richard Stutman, President
  180 Mt. Vernon Street, Boston, MA 02125
  Tel: 617.BTU.2000
  www.btu.org
  rstutman@btu.org

- **Clark University**
  Thomas Del Prete,[54] Director
  Jacob Hiatt Center for Urban Education
  Chair, Education Department
  Department of Education
  950 Main Street, Worcester, MA 01610
  Tel: 508.793.7197
  www.clark.edu
  tdelprete@clarku.edu

- **Worcester Public Schools**
  James Caradonio, Superintendent
  20 Irving Street, Worcester, MA 01609
  Tel: 508.799.3115   Fax: 508.799.3119
  www.wpsweb.com
  caradonio@worc.k12.ma.us

- **Educational Association of Worcester**
  Cheryl Del Signore, President
  397 Grove Street, Worcester, MA 01605
  Tel: 508.791.3296   Fax: 508.754.2461
  Worcester.massteacher.org
  cheryl.eaw@gmail.com

CHAPTER FOOTNOTES

32. Koppich, J. and Kerchner, C. (1997). United Mind Workers: Unions and Teaching in the Knowledge Society. San Francisco: Jossey-Bass Inc.

33. Tom Vander Ark, executive director for education at the Bill & Melinda Gates Foundation, is a major proponent of small schools and/or small learning communities within schools. Hill, D. (Oct. 10, 2001). Breaking Up Is Hard To Do. Education Week.

34. Meier, D.W. (1996). The Big Benefits of Smallness. Educational Leadership. 54.:1.

35. Several foundations are investing considerable resources in smaller learning communities. The Annenberg Foundation committed $500 million to reform urban high schools, emphasizing reduction in school size. In 2001, the Carnegie Foundation and Bill and Melinda Gates Foundation jointly established the 'Schools for a New Society' initiative with $60 million, to be matched locally. These monies were granted to Boston; Chattanooga, Tenn.; Providence, R.I.; Sacramento, Calif.; San Diego; and Worcester, Mass.. In addition, the Gates Foundation invested more that $600 million in 1,467 small high schools.

36. The public also supports the concept of smaller learning communities. The Public Agenda Foundation conducted a study of students, parents, and teachers, which found that parents are the most enthusiastic about small learning communities and that they perceive significant advantages to small high schools over large ones. Public Agenda Foundation (2002). Sizing Things Up: Small High Schools Get Thumbs Up From Parents. www.publicagenda.org/press. However, parents do not single out small schools as their highest priority in education reform. Foundation President Deborah Wadsworth believes that parents lack information about small learning communities.

37. www.ed.gov/programs/slcp/index.html

38. Tom Vander Ark of the Bill and Melinda Gates Foundation quoted in Hendrie, C. (June 16, 2004). High Schools Nationwide Paring Down. Education Week.

39. Lee, V.E., Smerdon, B.A., Alfreld-Liro, C., and Brown, S.L. (2000). Inside large and small high schools: Curriculum and social relations. Educational Evaluation and Policy Analysis. 22:2: 147-71.

40. Hill, D. (Oct. 10, 2001). Breaking up is hard to do. Education Week.

41. Bill and Melinda Gates Foundation, 2004. Education Program Fact Sheet. www.gatesfoundation.org/ mediacenter/publications

42. Valerie E. Lee and David T. Burkam quoted in "Do smaller structures help lower dropout risk?" Harvard Education Letter. March/April 2001.

43. Lawrence, B.K. et al. (2002). The cost effectiveness of small schools. Cincinnati: Knowledge Works Foundation.

44. National Center for Educational Statistics. (1998). Violence and discipline problems in U.S. public schools, 1996-1997. www.nces.ed.gov/pubs/violence

45. Research done on small learning communities in the 1990s generally did not address effects on achievement. The Bill and Melinda Gates Foundation has commissioned a comprehensive study of its investments in small schools from the American Institutes of Research and SRI International.

46. Howley, C. and Bickel, R. (2002). School size, poverty and student achievement. Washington, D.C.: The Rural School and Community Trust. Available: www.ruraled.org/docs/sapss/sapss.html

47. Darling-Hammond, L., Ancess, J., and Wichterle, S. (2002.). Reinventing high school: Outcomes of the Coalition Campus Schools Project. American Educational Research Journal. 39, 3, Pp. 639-673.

48. Center for Education Research and Policy at MassINC (2003). Head of the class: Characteristics of higher performing urban high schools in Massachusetts. Boston.

49. Ibid.

50. A full description of five small learning communities established in Boston can be found in: Allen, L., Almeida, C., and Steinberg, A. (2002). Wall to wall: Implementing small learning communities in five Boston high schools. Providence, R.I.: The Education Alliance at Brown University. Labor Working Paper No.3.

51. Head of the Class, Page 21.

52. Ibid, Page 25.

53. EAW and Worcester School Committee. Side Letter, Small Learning Communities. February 2003. The Side Letter is more extensively discussed in the section of this booklet on contract waivers and over-rides.

54. Thomas Del Prete coordinates the Carnegie project between the Carnegie Foundation and Worcester School District.

Improving Low Performance

Even before the passage of the No Child Left Behind Act, school districts and unions were addressing student performance shortfalls in collective-bargaining agreements. Contract language addressing the improvement of low-performing schools usually appears in the context of overall school accountability systems. This language represents a joint agreement to suspend "business as usual." The intent is to change the conditions in schools in order to focus the work of professionals in these schools, add resources, provide incentives for improvement, and define consequences if student performance does not get better. Support and incentives for high performance might include supplemental school resources, increased school autonomy, additional pay for teachers, and official recognition.

Three forms of interventions are described here: school designations based on performance that triggers new management conditions, school intervention processes, and innovative uses of time to improve outcomes.

SPECIAL DISTRICTS

Special administrative districts are formed through the segregation of a group of schools requiring special treatment and support. The imposition of these special districts is an accountability measure designed to help struggling schools improve quickly. Schools receive special designation in order to ensure that there is an ongoing effort to address pervasive performance problems. Most often, these performance problems are manifested by low or declining student achievement, but other poor outcomes such as high dropout rates may also characterize these schools. Accordingly, special management conditions are frequently the first line of defense against further decline, offering the beginnings of a strategic reform process focused on student success.

USEFULNESS TO IMPROVING STUDENT ACHIEVEMENT

Schools in these special administrative districts receive close management scrutiny as they come under centralized authority. The assumption guiding this practice is that scrutiny by a central authority will support schools that have demonstrated an inability to innovate or improve independently. In this way, schools with especially challenging circumstances receive specifically focused attention and resources to address their challenges.

CASE EXAMPLE:

Highly Structured Improvement Plan Laid Out for 'Chancellor's District'

NEW YORK, N.Y. In 1989, the New York State Education Department created a statewide list of Schools Under Registration Review (SURR) that identified the state's lowest-performing schools (as per achievement on Grade 4 and

Grade 8 English language arts and math assessments and similar high school assessments for high schools).[1] Once on the SURR list, a school must submit an improvement plan to the state education department. Additionally, the school must demonstrate significant improvement within three years or risk closure. New York City had 104 SURR schools on the original list.[2]

In 1996, then-New York City Chancellor Rudy Crew established a "virtual district" of 47 of the lowest-performing elementary and middle schools from the SURR list and placed them under the supervision of his office.

The intervening administrative structure organized around these low-performing schools was known as the "Chancellor's District," which reasserted central authority over the schools and imposed a highly structured improvement plan including the following:[3]

- Reduced class size

- Extended instructional day and school year

- After-school tutoring available until 6:00 pm for all students

- Structured reading curricula (Success for All and Balanced Literacy)

- Structured math curricula (Trailblazers)

- Daily schedule with two 90-minute blocks for literacy, a 60-minute block for math, and a 30-minute skill block alternating between literacy and math skills[4]

- Four, on-staff professional development experts at each school

- On-site teacher coaching center staffed by a teacher specialist

- One week of professional development for teachers every August

The United Federation of Teachers is described as "thoroughly committed to making sure" the special district worked.[5] The on-site teacher centers were run by the union and supported their

instructional approaches. The district and union negotiated terms to attract the most qualified teachers to schools in the Chancellor's District. Included were signing bonuses for certified teachers from private schools, as well as grants to meet the expense of earning a Master's degree toward certification or to repay educational loans.

Schools in the Chancellor's District also received high levels of scrutiny designed to improve their performance. They used regular assessment and made adjustments based on the analysis of this data. Schools that met performance targets were removed from the Chancellor's District and returned to their home districts. Schools that did not meet these targets were closed.

The Chancellor's District operated with its full program between academic year 1999-2000 and 2001-02. In those years, SURR elementary schools in the Chancellor's District outperformed other SURR schools on literacy assessments. Math scores improved, but did not overtake those of other SURR schools. The Chancellor's District was discontinued by the new chancellor in 2003, though elements remain for SURR schools. (See Extending the School Day and Year, Pg.109.)

CASE EXAMPLE:

Extended School Day and Year
Part of Plan for Struggling Schools

BALTIMORE. In 1997, the state of Maryland intervened in the Baltimore City Public School System (BCPSS) in response to pervasively poor student test scores, several lawsuits over special education provisions, and the inadequacy of K-12 funding.[6] The system was removed from the sole control of the mayor of Baltimore, and the school board was replaced with a Board of Commissioners, whose members were appointed by the governor, mayor, and state superintendent of education. The board was charged to come up with a five-year master plan to improve the system and to hire a chief executive officer.

Before a new CEO was hired, private education management companies were invited to bid for contracts to reconstitute the failing schools in Baltimore.[7] Edison Schools won the five-year contract and began management of three schools in 2000, though the teachers' union sued to cancel enforcement. This contract award was a blow to the union because Edison became the effective employer, with the right to hire, assign, and evaluate teachers, as well as to establish their pay scale. The state made it clear that it had the right to "terminate the contract with the union" at those three schools because of the poor performance of the students.[8]

CONTRACT LANGUAGE EXAMPLES

Agreement by and between the New Baltimore City Board of School Commissioners and the Baltimore Teachers Union Regarding the CEO District. March 20, 2001 through June 2004.

Staffing and Transfers
A Personnel Committee for the selection of teachers at each school in the District shall be established consisting of (i) one teacher Union representative designated by the BTU President, (ii) one representative designated by the BCPSS Chief Executive Officer (the "CEO"), (iii) the Principal of the school, and (iv) one Achievement First representative.

For the initial staff of each school in the District, and during subsequent school years, the Personnel Committee shall review all employment applications, interview candidates and make recommendations to the CEO for approval.

4. All Employees servicing in each school...shall have the option to apply for assignment in that school... shall be granted an interview upon request...

When Carmen Russo was hired as the new CEO in 2001, she established a "CEO District" for low-performing schools, proactively adding schools to the virtual district before they were officially reconstituted by the state. In the case of Westport Academy, a school the state nearly contracted to Edison, Russo arranged to re-open the bidding competition and selected Victory Schools to manage the school instead. Unlike the experience with Edison Schools, the Baltimore Teachers Union (BTU) was consulted during the process and entered into an agreement to cover this one school.[9] This agreement became the template for all CEO district schools.

The agreement covering schools in the CEO district provides:[10]

- An extended school day and year
- "Zero-based staffing" (no guaranteed position at the school)[11]
- Joint Personnel Committee (comprised of one representative of the CEO, principal, and union) for teacher selection at each school
- Performance awards for teachers if students' test scores improve by one-third of the points required to move out of reconstitution status[12]
- Bonuses for teachers with certifications in areas of need (or who earn certifications in these areas) and who volunteer to teach in CEO districts
- First opportunity to attract certified teachers to their schools

Using these provisions, schools in the CEO district were able to change the staffing composition of the schools, though a shortage of certified teachers remains. A survey of teachers conducted as part of a comprehensive evaluation of the state intervention shows that CEO district schools have attracted a committed group of teachers, 60 of whom claim that the "challenge and reward of working with children in an urban system" brought them to BCPSS. This percentage is higher than that reported by the teachers in other types of schools. Additionally, a greater percentage of them say they would recommend BCPSS to a friend as a place to work.[13]

Student achievement improved in CEO district schools within three years, as evidenced by the schools' median ranking on the TerraNova improving from the 28th to 36th percentile in reading and from 23rd to 38th percentile in math. Regular schools and CEO district schools experienced similar improvement in reading, but CEO district schools improved more in math than regular schools.

RESOURCES AND REFERENCES

- **United Federation of Teachers, New York City**
  Aminda Gentile, Director
  52 Broadway, 18th Floor, New York, NY 10004
  Tel. 212.475.3737   Fax. 212.475.9049
  www.ufttc.org

- **United Federation of Teachers, New York City**
  Carol Haupt, Teacher Center
  52 Broadway, 18th Floor, New York, NY 10004
  Tel. 212.475.3737   Fax.212.475.9049
  www.ufttc.org

- **American Federation of Teachers (Baltimore)**
  Joan Devlin, Associate Director, Education Issues
  555 New Jersey Avenue NW, Washington, D.C. 20001
  202.393.8642
  Jdevlin@aft.org

- **Baltimore Public School System**
  Bonnie S. Copeland, CEO
  200 East North Avenue, Baltimore, MD 21202
  410.396.8700

- **Baltimore City Public School System**
  Barbara Johnson, Principal, West Port Academy
  2401 Nevada Street, Baltimore, MD 21230
  410.396.3396

- **Baltimore Teachers Union**
  Marietta English, President
  5000 Metro Drive, 2nd Floor, Baltimore, MD 21215
  410.358.6600

CHAPTER FOOTNOTES

1. High schools are also evaluated on their dropout rates.

2. New York City has 1,200 public schools, now organized in nine sub-districts. Not all SURR schools are in the Chancellor's District.

3. For an analysis of the organizational theory behind this innovation, see Phenix, D.; Siegel, D.; Zaltsman, A.; and Fruchter, N. (2004). *Virtual district, real improvement: A retrospective evaluation of the Chancellor's District, 1996-2003.* New York: Institute for Education and Social Policy, Steinhardt School of Education, New York University.

4. This is the elementary school schedule. The middle school schedule was also highly structured around literacy.

5. Snipes, J.; Doolittle, F.; Herlihy, C. (2002). *Foundations*

for success: Case studies of how urban school systems improve student achievement. Washington, D.C.: Council of Great City Schools.

6. Senate Bill 795.

7. Maryland state law allows the Department of Education to contract directly or allow the local school system to contract with outside companies to manage schools under state intervention. In either case, the state supervises the school, monitoring its progress quarterly. See Maryland State Department of Education (2003). *School reconstitution: State intervention procedures for schools not progressing toward state standards.*

8. Bradley, A. Baltimore union sues to stop private firms from running schools. *Education Week.* May 3, 2000.

9. Agreement by and between the New Baltimore City Board of School Commissioners and the Baltimore Teachers Union Regarding the Reconstitution of Westport Elementary/Middle School #225." Feb. 20,

2001.

10. Agreement by and between the New Baltimore City Board of School Commissioners and the Baltimore Teachers Union Regarding the CEO District. March 20, 2001, through June 2004.

11. Morando Rhim, L. (2003). *Restructuring schools in Baltimore: An analysis of state and district efforts.* Washington, D.C.: Education Commission of the States policy brief. See www.ecs.org

12. Awards are equal to one step increase in service. Teachers with three years of service in CEO district schools are eligible for one step increases in service when their school improves enough so that it leave reconstitution status (pro rated).

13. Westat (2001). *Report on the final evaluation of the city-state partnership.* See www.bcps.k12.md.us

SCHOOL INTERVENTION PROCESSES

Intervention is a broad term, which does not always mean the same thing from district to district. However, in most instances, intervention entails at least a partial pre-emption of individual school autonomy by central district authority, as well as requiring a written plan and timeline for improvement, oversight, benchmarks, and expectations for improvement in student-oriented indicators.

Consequences for failure to improve—once an intervention process has run its course—vary, but they may include re-staffing, reorganization, or closure. Administrative interventions in the operations of a school almost always follow other, milder efforts to address unsatisfactory performance such as closer scrutiny by the district and the imposition of some sort of probationary status. These include a jointly drawn plan for remediation and technical assistance.

School intervention involves comprehensive analysis of a school's performance shortcomings and entails the design, implementation, and evaluation of reform efforts. This contrasts with the implementation of special districts, which is an administrative, structural reform intended to jump-start and monitor change.

USEFULNESS TO IMPROVING STUDENT ACHIEVEMENT

Contract language on intervention usually appears in the context of overall school accountability systems, and it is always focused on student achievement. Intervention processes represent the aggressive end of the accountability continuum. When a school is determined to be in need of intervention, it is performing poorly. Just as school success is often rewarded with increased autonomy and a looser administrative grip, performance failure frequently results in prescribed remediation, closer scrutiny, and specific expectations. School intervention processes, which involve the participation of teachers and their unions, are intended to bring greater perspective, capacity, and commitment to the results.

CASE EXAMPLE:

Continuum Identifies Schools At Different Achievement Levels

MINNEAPOLIS. Minneapolis identifies a "school performance management continuum" with three categories of schools qualifying for different treatment:

- **Development schools** are in good shape. They show steady gains in student achievement, narrowing of minority achievement gaps, and good learning climates.
- **Technical assistance schools** are those showing little improvement. Student achievement is poor and "stagnant." Achievement gaps remain steady, and the learning climates indicate "signs of trouble."
- **Intervention schools** are failing. Student achievement indicators are in decline. Achievement gaps for minority populations are widening, and the learning climate is negative, characterized by "dysfunction and denial."[14]

Article IV of the 2001-2003 Agreement between the Minneapolis Federation of Teachers and the Minneapolis Public School District is entitled: *Shared Leadership For Continuous Improvement.* Totaling 40 pages in length, this is by far the most extensive section of the 257-page agreement. Written in a narrative style, this section articulates that the goal of shared leadership is to improve the performance of all students, all schools, and the whole system.[15] Article IV is not subject to the grievance process.[16]

Accordingly, each school is expected to continuously renew itself and develop strategies to improve the achievement of each student served, while eliminating gaps in learning between groups of students. The shared leadership plan includes a site-level accountability system that has six parts, identified as tools and "components of a single and continuous improvement process at each school site." One part is a school improvement plan (SIP). Significantly, the shared leadership plan applies to all schools, not just low-performing schools.[17] However, when schools fall into a category indicating less than satisfactory performance on the school performance continuum, special management conditions apply.

The first phase of special management entails the provision of support. Primarily, schools receive help in the form of technical services from the district and are subject to oversight by a "Core Team" with representatives from the school's leadership team, the superintendent's office, a principals' group, and perhaps others that could include the state Department of Children, Families and Learning. An action plan is formulated, a timeline is established, and results are monitored. Examples of services that might be offered to schools undergoing technical assistance include additional time and/or resources for staff development, challenge grants, climate surveys, and extra support for students.[18]

When struggling schools in Minneapolis have been through the "support and technical assistance" phase of the accountability system and failed to make satisfactory progress, they enter intervention. Intervention begins with identification of the school's strengths and most pressing needs. Then, the district collaborates with a school leadership team to develop a strategy for correction. Strict expectations and timelines are stated.

Next, the school staff is given an opportunity to choose from among several team-approved research-based improvement models as the basis for implementing the approved strategy. The district assumes responsibility for making certain that staff members have the information and resources they need to make an informed choice. Accordingly, teachers are furnished with material concerning research results for the various models under consideration, including the costs of implementation, curriculum materials required, and professional development demands that may be placed upon them. They are given opportunities to visit other schools where the models are in place. Significantly—after a reform model has been selected—teachers who are unwilling to commit their full effort to the intervention process are given an opportunity to transfer out of the site. They can be reassigned to other duties within the district in accordance with the general provisions of the agreement.[19]

Minneapolis has adopted a point system for measuring individual school progress in all stages of accountability. Quality indicators include student achievement, school climate, attendance and suspension rates, and gifted/talented programming. Point scores range from one (low) to five (high).[20] The contract also contains tables that are tools for implementing and tracking reform initiatives. They identify topic areas, define responsibility, and state decision-making parameters.[21]

CASE EXAMPLE:

School Plans Must Emphasize Six Essentials for Improvement

BOSTON. In Boston, schools with unsatisfactory student achievement results move immediately into a special management arena designed to identify issues, provide assistance, and monitor results.

Article IV of the 2003-2006 agreement between the Boston Teachers Union and the Boston School Committee requires that every Boston school prepare a written Whole School Improvement Plan every year. The primary purpose of the plan is to provide the leadership of each school with a process to help guide its decision-making regarding instructional improvement and programmatic options offered to students. Plans are designed to enable those in schools and support to identify the extent to which the school is adding value to learners' prior abilities and skills.[22]

Whole School Improvement Plans are required to be guided and built on six essentials for school improvement:

- Use effective instructional practices and create a collaborative school climate to improve student learning
- Examine student work and data to drive instruction and professional development
- Invest in professional development to improve instruction
- Share leadership to sustain instructional improvement
- Focus resources to support instructional improvement and improved student learning
- Partner with families and community to support student learning[23]

Schools are assessed annually. Each school must undergo a rigorous external review by the deputy superintendent comparing goals outlined in the Whole School Improvement Plan with actual performance. A school whose performance is determined to be unsatisfactory may be subject to fuller review by a labor-management intervention team convened by the superintendent. The team assesses the reasons for underperformance and prepares a revised plan that is submitted to the superintendent for action.[24]

When a school is designated as underperforming, the superintendent gains certain extraordinary authority, including the right to fill up to 50 percent of all vacancies and the right to require teachers to participate in up to 20 hours of additional professional development. Remedial plans can also recommend the removal of a BTU building representative from an under-performing school. Implementation of this recommendation requires a meeting between the superintendent and the president of the Boston Teachers Union, as well as their agreement to the removal.[25]

Annual assessments are not subject to the grievance procedures. A school can request review of an assessment result by the deputy superintendent, but only the superintendent has the authority to change an assessment.[26]

CASE EXAMPLE:

Progress Assessments Target Achievement, School Quality

ROCHESTER, N.Y. Rochester has implemented an accountability system that includes three "phases"—*incentive, intervention,* and *sanction*—which are really categories into which every school is placed.

Section 55 of the July 1, 2002, agreement between the Rochester Teachers Association and the City School District of Rochester describes a system of accountability similar to those in Minneapolis and Boston in that it includes mandatory school accountability plans for all schools (or small learning communities), not just those that are low performing. Among other things, the agreement requires that school success be measured on the basis of student outcomes, and that annual progress assessments must occur. Progress assessments address student achievement and school quality indicators. Student achievement takes into account test scores, readiness of students to advance to the next grade levels, feedback from receiving schools, writing skills, and more. School quality indicators include (but are not limited to) parent involvement and "customer satisfaction."[27] Improvement plans will be modified from year to year in response to evidence of effective strategies revealed by assessments.

Schools (or small learning communities) that demonstrate success in achieving the goals of their accountability plans are rewarded with greater

---

CONTRACT LANGUAGE EXAMPLES

2003-2005 Agreement between the Minneapolis Board of Education and the Minneapolis Federation of Teachers. Article IV, page 46.

The Intervention Stage: For sites in which the outcomes from the Support and Technical Assistance Stage of District services do not result in satisfactory and sustained progress on the School Performance Continuum, the school enters the intervention Stage of District services. The core team may be formed again according to the site's specific needs

Implementing effective school wide improvement is a massive undertaking because it touches upon all areas of a school's culture and practice. To achieve whole school reform and improvement, educators must tackle a comprehensive set of initiatives, including appropriate professional development, high quality curricula, and a number of other organizational changes.

2003-2006 Collective Bargaining Agreement between the Boston Teachers Union and the Boston School Committee. Article IV, C.

The School Intervention Team will be composed of three members selected by the Union, three members selected by the Superintendent and a seventh member who is jointly agreed to by the Superintendent and the President of the Union…This team will initiate an assessment of the reasons for the under-performance and present a remedial plan for improvement after spending time in the school and talking with school staff, parents and community members. The remedial plan will be completed up to four months after the team is appointed. The plan will then be submitted to the Superintendent for appropriate action.

autonomy, flexibility, recognition, and additional resources, as well as increased discretion in the use of resources. Schools (or small learning communities) that fail to succeed in achieving the goals of their accountability plans face "logical consequences," and are moved to the intervention phase of accountability.[28]

In Rochester, the school performance accountability system includes an *intervention* phase and a *sanction* phase. The intervention phase comes first and is triggered when a school fails to demonstrate satisfactory progress in the annual accountability plan assessment process.[29]

The intervention process is primarily remedial. It offers outside assistance and the opportunity for critical review of existing programs and practices affecting school performance and student achievement. A school under intervention must participate in a review process that focuses on areas in need of improvement and involves the creation of an improvement plan "based on findings; prescribed professional development such as visitations to schools which have demonstrated success; changes in procedures and/or school operations; audits of student work and monitoring of school efforts."[30] Schools that demonstrate improvement in the two-year intervention period are monitored for a third year, and if improvement continues, they are removed from intervention. Schools that do not show satisfactory improvement during the first two years of intervention move to the more serious sanction phase of the accountability process.

In the sanction phase, the district appoints a "monitor" to work with a school-based Planning Steering Committee toward improvement. Sanctions include various consequences, including imposed staffing changes, replacement or reconstituting of programs, and school closing. Schools that do not show improvement for a total of five years—which may be the intervention phase tacked on to the sanction phase—must at least be restructured. Schools that emerge from the sanction phase continue to be monitored as if they

were in the intervention phase for some period of time, to be determined by a school-based Planning Steering Committee.

CASE EXAMPLE:

Denver Targets Collaboration, Unique Needs of Pupils

DENVER. In their 2002-2005 "Agreement and Partnership," the Denver Teachers Association and the Denver School District established Collaborative Decision Making (CDM).[31] Accordingly, staff, parents, and community members—in each school—work together to create and implement a school improvement plan (SIP) focused on the unique needs of students in that school. The SIP is a guideline for meeting student achievement and behavior goals as stated by the district. It is not necessarily remedial and is not specific to low-performing schools.

Among other things, the CDM committee is required to "assess the satisfaction of the school community with the school" by conducting a survey of school constituents, including parents and community members, students, staff, and teachers. Items covered must include academic achievement, the effectiveness of principals and teachers, and the overall climate of the school.[32]

CASE EXAMPLE:

Toledo Agreement Stresses Union, District Cooperation

TOLEDO, OHIO. Article XXV of the 2001-2004 agreement between the Toledo Federation of Teachers and the Toledo Public Schools is entitled School Intervention Team. It is short and isolated within the agreement; there is no context. The article simply calls for collaboration between the district and the union. It states that a joint team appointed by both shall be given responsibility for the improvement of a school's operation, and that the team will construct guidelines for changes and monitor the results.[33]

Appendix W to the same agreement is entitled School Improvement Plans. It contains a section on Individual School Building Goals and requires that each school in the district develop a School Improvement Plan "to address the goals established by the Board of Education and needs identified at the buildings."

OTHER EXAMPLES OF DISTRICTS WITH SCHOOL INTERVENTION PROCESSES

- Cincinnati
- Dade County, Fla.
- New York, N.Y.
- Providence, R.I.
- San Diego
- Seattle

CHAPTER FOOTNOTES

14. 2001-2003 Agreement between the Minneapolis Federation of Teachers and the Minneapolis Public School District. Page 45 and Article IV Addendum at Page 52.

15. Ibid. Page 21.

16. Ibid. Page 51.

17. The School Improvement Process (SIP) is described in 2001-2003 Agreement between the Minneapolis Federation of Teachers and the Minneapolis Public School District. Section D, Page 34.

18. Ibid. Page 47.

19. The contract states: "since staff support is critical for the effective implementation of a successful academic plan, any staff member who prefers not to work with the adopted model will be allowed to transfer under the transfer and reassignment provisions of this contract, and a team of teachers with training and experience in the selected model will be recruited into the school."

20. 2001-2003 Agreement between the Minneapolis Federation of Teachers and the Minneapolis Public School District. Section D, Page 49.

21. Ibid. Pp. 52-60.

22. See 2003-2006 Agreement between the Boston Teachers Union and the Boston School Committee, Article IV A-3.

23. Ibid. Page 31.

24. Ibid. Article IV C.

25. Ibid. Article IV D.

26. Ibid. Article IV B-2.

27. July 1, 2002. Agreement between the City School District of Rochester and the Rochester Teachers Association. Section 55.

28. July 2002. Agreement between the City School District of Rochester and the Rochester Teachers Association. Section 55.

29. July 2002. Agreement between the City School District of Rochester and the Rochester Teachers Association, Section 55 E.

30. Ibid, Page 116.

31. 2002-2005 Agreement and Partnership Between School District No. 1 and Denver Classroom Teachers Association, Article 5.

32. Ibid. Article 5-10.

33. Despite the reference to intervention, in the context of this discussion the Toledo contract language falls more under the category of Special Management Conditions than School Intervention Processes.

RESOURCES AND REFERENCES

- **Boston Public Schools**
  Thomas Payzant, Superintendent
  26 Court Street, Boston, MA 02108
  Tel: 617.635.9050
  www.boston.k12.ma.us

- **Boston Teachers Union**
  Richard Stutman, President
  180 Mt. Vernon Street, Boston, MA 02125
  Tel: 617.BTU.2000
  www.btu.org
  rstutman@btu.org

- **Denver Public Schools**
  Andre Pettigrew, Assistant Superintendent
  Administrative Services
  900 Grant Street, Denver, CO 80203
  Tel: 303.764.3296
  www.denver.k12.com
  andre_pettigrew@dpsk12.org

- **Denver Classroom Teachers Association**
  Becky Wissink, President
  150 Grant Street, Suite 200, Denver, CO 80203
  Tel: 303.831.0590   Fax: 303.831.0591
  bwissink@nea.org

- **Minneapolis Public Schools**
  Patricia Thornton, Coordinator
  College-School Collaborations in Teacher Development
  159 Pillsbury Drive SE, Minneapolis, MN 55455
  Tel: 612.625.8974   Fax: 612.624.8744
  kalni001@tc.umn.edu

- **Minneapolis Federation of Teachers**
  Louise Sundin, President
  67 8th Avenue, NE, Minneapolis, MN 55413
  Tel: 612.529.9621
  www.MFT59.org

- **Rochester Public Schools**
  Manuel J. Rivera, Superintendent
  131 West Broad Street, Rochester, NY 14614
  Tel: 585.262 8100
  www.rcsdk12.org
  manuel.rivera@rcsdk12.org

- **Rochester Teachers Association**
  Adam Urbanski, President
  30 N. Union Street, Suite 301, Rochester, NY 14607
  Tel: 585.546.2681
  www.rochesterteachers.com
  urbanski@rochesterteachers.com

- **Toledo Federation of Teachers**
  Francine Lawrence, President
  111 S. Byrne Road, Toledo, OH 43615
  Tel: 419.535.3013
  www.tft250.org

- **Toledo Public Schools**
  Eugene T.W. Sanders, Superintendent
  420 E. Manhattan Boulevard, Toledo, OH 43608
  Tel: 419.729.8200

- **Toledo Public Schools**
  Craig Cotner, Chief Academic Officer
  420 E. Manhattan Boulevard, Toledo, OH 43608
  Tel: 419.729.8422
  craig.cotner@tps.org

EXTENDING THE SCHOOL DAY AND YEAR

Research shows that both the amount and scheduling of "learning time" impacts student achievement.[34] Acknowledging the relationship between time spent in school and student learning, all states but one define the minimum number of days or hours in the academic calendar. Because time is manageable and measurable, teacher contracts typically speak to time issues with great specificity, defining both the length of the school day and the use of time during that defined day.

USEFULNESS TO IMPROVING STUDENT ACHIEVEMENT

Extending the school day or school year provides educators with the flexibility needed to structure more effective instruction. In response, some districts have opted to increase the required number of in-school hours, reduce non-academic time, and/or reduce the time between instructional experiences. Other districts have maintained the same number of academic school days, but have modified their calendars to avoid the long vacations, which result in learning loss among at-risk students. Through these strategies, instructional time is extended or rescheduled, providing educators with a better opportunity to focus on addressing students' special needs and learning styles.

Within the existing system, several factors impede effective scheduling and use of in-school learning time. "One-size-fits-all" schedules make it difficult to teach students at different achievement levels. Traditional schedules do not correspond with how many students learn best: in small groups and with continuity. Additionally, in-school learning time is sometimes lost to "administrivia," non-instructional activities or, ironically, professional development. Lengthy summer holidays and school breaks further reduce possible time spent in school.

While increasing in-school time raises myriad financial, social, and policy challenges, there is evidence that better use of available time is effective in improving the performance of schools with a large portion of at-risk students.[35] In considering this issue, questions have been raised regarding:

- The proportion of the school year and school day spent on instruction
- Whether instructional time tracks the way children learn, and
- The detrimental impact of school breaks on learning retention[36]

Both the quantity and coordination of in-school time have been the focus of education reform discussion. Since publication of *A Nation at Risk* in 1983, which called for lengthening the school year to 210 days, much emphasis has been placed on international comparisons of school day and calendar length.[37] However, another pertinent, nationally focused question has been raised: "Are U.S. students in school for enough time to learn what is required by state standards?"[38]

In response, researchers now differentiate between three different measures of time:[39]

- **Allocated time** — the aggregate number of hours students are in school;

- **Engaged time** — the number of hours students are engaged in instruction; and

- **Learning time** — the subset of hours of instructional time when academic learning occurs.

   Imagining the three types of time as a hierarchy, it is clear that "learning time" is a subset of the first two and the smallest of them. Much of the time students are in school (allocated time) is not used for instruction. Assemblies, special holiday activities, and other "distractions" from curriculum reduce overall time for learning. Scheduled instructional periods (engaged time) are not spent optimally. Interruptions in the continuity of "learning time" by all school public address systems, pull-outs, and professional development days all contribute to breaking up learning time. Even when they are not interrupted by external activities, teachers spend a considerable amount of instructional time on administrative activities such as record-keeping and report-writing.

   Learning time may not be scheduled optimally or paced correctly for the material being taught or the developmental stage of the learners. The debate over the optimal length of time blocks for learning has been overshadowed by new calls to match the length and pacing of learning time with the learning style or stage of development of the learner. This would in effect create a schedule where "time should be adjusted to meet the individual needs of learners, rather than the administrative convenience of adults."[40] In practice, flexibility in scheduling would allow more team teaching, team learning, ability groupings, and individual attention, among other innovations.

   In addition, recent research suggests that the lengthy summer vacation enjoyed by U.S. students may be problematic for at-risk students. All students experience setbacks in math knowledge as a result of the summer vacation. Reading, however, is a different story. While middle-class children make gains during the summer in reading ability, poor and disadvantaged children typically lose between one and three months on a grade-level-equivalent scale.[41] As the grades progress, the negative effect of summer breaks increases, and the gap between middle-class and poor kids increases as well. There are some estimates that show the difference between the achievement of advantaged and disadvantaged high school students is largely explained by the "summer" effects.[42] Teachers in schools where the regular number of academic days is distributed over a calendar year and vacation periods are shorter than normal spend less time reviewing material from earlier units, allowing them more time for new instruction. In addition, there is some evidence from a Canadian experiment that an extended calendar improves attendance and lowers dropout rates.

   Innovative efforts have been made to extend the school day or school year to accommodate all scheduled activities (including professional development) and to increase scheduling flexibility. These innovations have required changes in collective-bargaining agreements that traditionally have focused on controlling the way time is used in minute detail.

CASE EXAMPLE:

Supplemental Pay Plan Covers Teachers in Extended Day Schools

NEW YORK, N.Y. The United Federation of Teachers (UFT) and the New York City School District have designated 51 low-performing schools (that are officially Schools Under Registration Review) as *extended time schools* in order to implement certain scheduling reforms aimed at improving student achievement. These schools have added time to the school day for professional development and small group instruction, while implementing research-based reform curricula and reducing class size.[43]

Teachers who serve in extended time schools are compensated for their extra time through a negotiated, supplemental pay schedule.[44] Teachers who are already on staff in schools at the time they are designated as extended time schools have the option of transferring to other schools. Some teachers may be involuntarily transferred out, in which case they have the opportunity to apply for a vacancy in another extended time school or to a regular schedule school in the district. However, no teacher can be involuntarily transferred into an extended school. Teachers who serve in extended time schools must agree to remain there for at least three years. If a teacher fails to do so, unless the school is taken off the extended-school list, he or she must reimburse the district for additional compensation received as a result of their extended school service.[45]

Extended time schools have unique features that sometimes require changes to the master agreement. It takes a lesser number of yes votes from union members to consent to any such change than is mandated for any school-based contract change in a non-extended school.[46]

Concerning professional development, the UFT president and the chancellor created a *Menu of Professional Activity Options* specific to extended time schools. The chancellor has special authority to direct specific professional development activities during designated professional development periods in extended time schools.[47]

Students in extended time schools have made more academic gains than their counterparts in schools with similar characteristics but traditional schedules. In May 2002, the New York Division of Accountability and Assessment confirmed that, for the second academic year, extended time schools improved at a greater rate on city and state English language arts and mathematics assessments than did students in non-extended-day schools. Most importantly, gains were made among students performing at the lowest proficiency level.[48]

In addition to extended time schools, New York has created *secondary opportunity schools* (SOS) to provide year-round instruction to students. Teachers in SOS work a regular school year (September through June) and may have extended duties during that period, for which they are compensated on a pro-rated basis. They must also work for not less than 30 days during July and August, at which time a workday consists of four-and-a-half hours, without lunch. As in extended time schools, SOS teachers must apply to serve in the program, and no teacher will be forced to participate. However, teachers who do apply for SOS must commit to remain in the district (not necessarily the program) for at least three years following acceptance into SOS.[49]

CASE EXAMPLE:

Year-Round Schooling Spreads Vacation Time Through Year

CHICAGO. In Chicago, 14 year-round schools were created. Neither the length nor the number of school days was increased. Instead, vacation time was spread throughout the year to create shorter and more frequent breaks.[50] The primary goals of the program were to avoid student-learning loss that normally occurs over the summers and to reduce teacher burnout. Other goals cited by the district are improved time management and planning opportunities for teachers, better teacher and student attendance, and better opportunities for student remediation.[51]

The district cites the following program accomplishments:

- Improved math and reading scores
- Lower teacher and student absenteeism rates
- More early intervention programs
- Improved relationships between teachers and students
- The elimination of overcrowding

Half of the 14 year-rounds schools have the same schedule, so that their students and teachers have breaks at the same time. The other year-round schools have staggered schedules designed to relieve overcrowding in buildings.

The year-round school program in Chicago is not part of the negotiated agreement between the board and the Chicago Teachers Union. Still, some year-round staffing issues are addressed in the agreement, including the rights of year-round teachers to substitute in regular schools during the year-round school's intercession.[52]

CASE EXAMPLE:

Baltimore 'CEO' Plan Includes Extended Days and Years

BALTIMORE. Baltimore has created a "CEO" district, consisting of 10 previously low-performing schools. One main feature of CEO district schools is that they all have extended days and extended academic years. These schools have other unique features as well, many of which had to be agreed upon by the district and the union, since they require departure from the master agreement. The initial assignment of teachers to CEO district schools was one of the most controversial matters addressed by the parties since this varies from the

normal seniority provisions of the contract. CEO schools each have specific goals for student achievement in the form of benchmarks, and teachers in schools that achieve their goals are rewarded with bonuses.[53]

As in Chicago, the CEO program is not referenced in the master agreement between the union and the district, but it appears in an amendment to the master agreement. The amendment is brief—only four pages long—and contains sections on staffing, performance incentives, and "extended day/professional development."[54]

CONTRACT LANGUAGE

2000-2003 Agreement Between The Board of Education of the City School District of the City of New York and The United Federation of Teachers. Article 12 II.

In order to raise student performance, the Chancellor has designated certain SURR (Schools Under Registration Review) and low performing schools as "Extended Time Schools" in which there will be an extended school day/year. The parties believe that implementation of this extended school schedule over a two year period will succeed in turning around low performing schools and having them removed from the SURR list....

All Extended Time Schools will operate pursuant to the School-Based Option Transfer and Staffing Plan, without an annual requirement to apply for participation.

Individual employees in Extended Time Schools will be required to sign a document agreeing to the terms

OTHER EXAMPLES OF DISTRICTS
WITH EXTENDED DAYS OR YEARS:

- Hillsborough, Fla.
- New Britain, Conn.

and conditions described herein.

The Board official(s) with responsibility for this program shall meet and consult at times mutually agreed with representatives of the union on matters of policy and implementation of the Extended Time Schools program.

Except as otherwise set forth herein, the terms and conditions of this collective bargaining agreement apply to employees serving in the Extended Time Schools program.

2/20/01 Amendment Agreement between the New Baltimore City Board of School Commissioners and the Baltimore Teachers Union, regarding the Reconstitution of Westport Elementary/Middle School #225. Article IV.

The parties agree that an extended day and extended year with additional compensation provided to Employees, is in their collective best interests, and the best interests of the School's children. The parties will negotiate in good faith to reach an extended day and extended year agreement, provided sufficient funding is available.

3/20/01 Amendment Agreement Between The New Baltimore City Board of School Commissioners and The Baltimore Teachers Union, regarding the CEO's District. Article IV.

Extended Day/Professional Development

Employees shall be expected to attend staff development seven days prior to the beginning of the school year, and shall be compensated as follows: Teachers shall receive $130 daily stipend for a maximum of six hours each of the seven days; Paraprofessionals shall receive their hourly rate for a minimum of five hours for each of the seven days.

Employees shall be expected to work an additional 50 minutes each day. Compensation for the extended day shall be at the rate of 11% increase to each Employee's base salary. Employees who transfer to schools outside the district shall not maintain the 11% increase upon transfer.

RESOURCES AND REFERENCES

- **Baltimore County Public Schools**
  Joe A. Hairston, Superintendent
  Greenwood Campus
  6901 North Charles Street, Towson, MD 21204
  Tel: 410.887.4281
  www.bcps.org

- **Baltimore Teachers Union**
  Marietta A. English, President
  Teacher Chapter
  5800 Metro Drive, Baltimore, MD 21215
  Tel: 410.358.6600
  www.baltu.org

- **American Federation of Teachers (Baltimore)**
  Joan Devlin, Associate Director
  Education Issues
  555 New Jersey Avenue NW, Washington, D.C. 20001
  Tel:202.393.8642
  Jdevlin@aft.org

- **Chicago Board of Education**
  125 So. Clark Street, Chicago, IL 60603
  Tel: 773.553.1600

- **Chicago Teachers Union**
  Allen E. Beardon, Director
  John Franz, Chief Labor Relations Officer
  222 Merchandise Mart Plaza, Suite 400, Chicago, IL 60654
  Tel: 312.329.9100
  www.ctunet.com

- **New York City Department of Education**
  Joel I. Klein, Chancellor
  52 Chamber Street, New York, NY10007
  Tel: 718.935.2000
  www.nycenet.edu

- **New York City United Federation of Teachers**
  Randi Weingarten, President
  52 Broadway Avenue, New York, NY 10004
  Tel: 212.777.7500

CHAPTER FOOTNOTES

34. Research shows small but positive correlations between time and achievement. It has been argued that small effects over a short period may aggregate much larger effects over time. In addition, there is evidence from evaluations of extended-time schools that shows a favorable impact on low-performing schools and the lowest-performing students, making these innovations important tools.

35. For example, in comparing schools with varying degrees of effectiveness, the Kentucky State Department of Education found that teachers in the better-performing schools spent more minutes on instruction, more time on student-led activities, and paced instruction more appropriately than did teachers in the lower-performing schools. For more, see: Meehan, M. L.; Cowley, K. S.; Schumacher, D.; Hauser, B.; Croom, N. D. M. (2003). *Classroom environment, instructional resources, and teaching differences in high-performing Kentucky schools with achievement gaps.* Louisville, Ky.: Paper Presented at the 12th Annual CREATE National Evaluation Institute.

36. See National Commission on Time and Learning (1994). *Prisoners of time.* Washington, D.C. www.ed.gov/pubs/PrisonersOfTime/index/html.

37. See Barrett, M. (1990). The case for more school days. *The Atlantic Monthly.*

38. When asked to estimate the amount of time required to teach average students to a defined benchmark within state standards at four grade levels, teachers in three states judged that they needed one-and-a-half times as many hours than the amount of time available for instruction. For more, see: Florian, J. (1999). *Teacher survey of standards-based instruction: Addressing time.* Colorado: Mid-Continent Research for Education and Learning. www.mcrel.org

39. Aronson, J., Zimmerman, J. and Carlos, L. (no date). *Improving student achievement by extending school: Is it just a matter of time?* Oakland, Calif.: Wested. www.wested.org/online_pubs/timeandlearning/htm

40. See National Commission on Time and Learning (1994). *Prisoners of time.* Washington, D.C. www.ed.gov/pubs/PrisonersOfTime/index/html.

41. Cooper, H. et al. (1996). The effects of summer vacation on achievement test score: A narrative and meta-analytic review. *Review of Education Research*, 66, 3, 3.

42. Entwisle, D. et al. (2001). Keep the faucet flowing: Summer learning and home environment. *American Educator.*

43. American Federation of Teachers (2000). *Doing what works: Improving big city schools.* Educational Issues Policy Brief. Washington, D.C.: Author. See http://aft.org/pubs-reports/downloads/teachers/policy12.pdf

44. Teachers work a seven-hour workday, including a duty-free lunch period, and an additional five workdays immediately before the beginning of the school year. Teachers are compensated for additional time in accordance with a negotiated salary schedule. 2000-2003 Agreement between the Board of Education of the City School District of New York and United Federation of Teachers, Article 12 II A.

45. 2000-2003 Agreement between the Board of Education of the City School District of New York and United Federation of Teachers, Article 12 II, Sections B and C.

46. Operational matters include class size, rotation of assignments/classes, teacher schedules, and/or rotation of paid coverage for the school year.

47. 2000-2003 Agreement between the Board of Education of the City School District of New York and United Federation of Teachers, Article 12 II, Section D.

48. New York City Board of Education, Division of Assessment and Accountability. "Two Year Analyses of Performance of Extended-Time and Non-Extended Time SURR Schools." Flash Research Report #7. May 2002.

49. 2000-2003 Agreement between the Board of Education of the City School District of New York and United Federation of Teachers, Article 12 III.

50. Children attend the mandatory 180 days per year, but the days are spread out so there are mini-breaks, or intersessions, throughout the year.

51. CPS Web site: http://www.cps.k12.il.us/yearroundschools

52. 1999-2003 Agreement between Board of Education of Chicago and Chicago Teachers Union. Article 14.

53. Feb. 20, 2004, telephone interview with Joan Devlin.

54. March 20, 2001, Agreement By and Between the New Baltimore City Board of School Commissioners and the Baltimore Teachers Union, American Federation of Teachers, Local #340 Regarding the CEO's District.

Partnering
and Networks

Partnership development is an increasingly common trend in public education that often helps school and district management and teachers' unions develop stronger working relationships focused on improving student achievement. At times, partnerships and less formal collaborations expand beyond district management and teachers' unions to include external stakeholder groups—universities, businesses, non-profit organizations, etc. Partnership trends reflect acceptance that the complexity of large-scale school reform entails input, expertise, and problem-solving from diverse stakeholders, not just school or district administrative leaders.[1]

The raw politics of education reform require partnering. It is virtually impossible to mount a significant change effort without stimulating the concern of the union and its members. Even when they support the ultimate reform goal, internal stakeholder groups (such as teachers' unions) have their own interests and

will want to ensure that these interests are aligned with reform efforts. Administrators and unions are also aware that when a collective-bargaining agreement is in place change may require negotiation about implementation and impacts.[2]

For both school administrators and the union, engagement is a more effective option than neutrality or passivity. Acting alone, administrators risk alienating teachers within their schools and developing unilateral, possibly ineffective, policies that lack teacher buy-in. From the union perspective, passivity may lead to the union's relegation and irrelevancy on issues that are important to their members.[3] The union will either be a full partner or a committed opponent, but in either role it will be present and active.

Public confidence in public education has eroded, and there is little patience for battles between stakeholder groups[4]. In this context, partnering serves to improve public perception when education professionals lead constructive change through collaboration. Given that public organizations are no longer trusted to fix their own problems, the perceived importance of partnering is even more real. Increasingly, a public institution's perceived legitimacy is linked to external relationships with non-public institutions.[5] For this reason, as well as to address capacity needs, schools and districts have increasingly engaged with institutions such as universities, community groups, and other districts to obtain needed resources and expertise.

Lastly, education reform is fundamentally about changing what happens between students and teachers. Efforts to change this intensely human interaction will create fear, loss, confusion, and conflict – all powerful emotions.[6] Where changes in professional practice are required but can't be closely supervised or monitored, the new norms and behaviors must eventually be internalized and monitored by the practitioners themselves. By their very nature, these are inclusive processes. Teacher inclusion in the reform process may occur at different points — at an early stage with the analysis of problems or later with the development and implementation of new practices. Teachers' reactions to reform will likely be affected by the extent to which they have been involved from an early stage in change efforts.

STRATEGIC PARTNERSHIPS

Strategic partnerships between labor and management often result in formal sharing of governance and authority in areas such as curriculum, finance, and professional development. Partnering represents a transition from an adversarial labor relations model to a collegial model in which professionals on both sides of the table share a common dedication and responsibility for student outcomes. Absent strategic partnerships, institutional responsibility for student outcomes resides with management, while unions are not required to assume responsibility for student achievement.

USEFULNESS TO IMPROVING STUDENT ACHIEVEMENT

Partnering changes the nature of the relationship between teachers' unions and management, focusing their collective work on organizational outcomes, including student achievement. The role of each party changes, too, when the parties recognize that they are interdependent and jointly responsible for ensuring student success in an age of accountability and competition.[8]

The traditional collective-bargaining relationship focuses on operational procedure in the workplace and the distribution of resources—with the employer exercising bureaucratic control through rules and the union "faithfully monitoring the uniformity of rule application, when those rules affect the conditions of employment or the ways in which employees are compensated, evaluated, or assigned to duties."[9] Employers, through the monopolization of discretion and authority, not only withhold opportunities to participate in decision-making, but they provide the union the safety of detached distance from the decision itself. "Don't blame us, we had nothing to do with this," the union can say to its members and to the public.

In stark contrast, the partnerships described in this section outline ways in which administrators and the union have innovated to share responsibility for decisions and the operation of strategies to improve student achievement. The unions in these examples have assumed responsibility for student achievement when their legal obligations do not require this. As a full partner in the governance of programs, the union is not able to distance itself from a program or from the outcomes of a program. Likewise, management has expanded the scope of topics that it is willing to address jointly with the union.

The nature of partnerships requires that each party must pay attention to the needs and concerns of the other party, but most importantly it entails maintaining a clear, joint focus on the primary goal of the working relationship— improving student achievement. Working together allows reframing of problems and a broadening of the search for solutions. The relationship is not a license to avoid doing the hard work of adapting work processes, policies, and procedures to the needs of the new environment. Neither does it mean that every decision and action is equally desirable or the result of a consensus. The goal is to find ways to improve the organization's performance within a framework that addresses the concerns and interests of both parties to the greatest extent possible. The focus on concerns and interests allows consideration of proposals that would never otherwise reach the light of day.

In the best circumstances, partnerships model commitment through leaders' face-to-face relationships. This commitment then carries over to institutional arrangements and downward to relationships between representatives of the parties at the school level. The commitment is recognized and made visible to all parties.

Strategic partnerships often begin with problem-solving activities at the workplace level or through personal relationships between administrative and union leaders. Over time, partnerships begin to address strategic issues involving joint governance and shared authority in specific functional areas crucial to the performance of the organizations. Partnerships may operate as a governance body at the district level, authorizing joint problem-solving activities in functional areas or at the school level.[10] The partnership may be institutionalized in agreements or memoranda of understanding and

may vary in their level of complexity.[11]

Strategic partnerships frequently take the form of joint committees, which focus on specific issues or areas of operation. For example, Denver has joint task forces on compensation and school climate.[12] In many cases there is a joint written statement of commitment by the district and the union to work together in reform efforts focused on student achievement.

CASE EXAMPLE:

Three-Year Agreement Empowers Union-District Steering Panel

BOSTON. The 2003-2006 agreement between the Boston Teachers Union (BTU) and the Boston School Committee creates a Union-School Department Steering Committee that is charged in part to "oversee the implementation and operation of school-based management/shared decision-making and all other joint committees established under this Agreement." Committee membership includes the superintendent and the union president, who have equal status as co-chairs. The committee may be comprised of up to 10 other members—five representing the administration and five representing the union. The committee has the authority to appoint subcommittees and task forces tailored to particular issues as they arise. The committee is meant to act on a consensus basis, and it can take no action unless the superintendent and the union president agree.[13]

The agreement allows for the formation of Faculty Senates in each school building. Senates are entitled to meet with building administrators on a regular basis. They are to be recognized by administrators as having an advisory voice in the operations of the school, as well as in the formation of educational policy for the school.[14]

The agreement also calls for the establishment of School Site Councils in every school, to be monitored by the steering committee. School Site

Councils are bound to operate within the terms of the collective-bargaining agreement in seeking solutions to problems in the schools and are charged to work collaboratively "to find good solutions to educational problems confronting the school."[15]

CASE EXAMPLE:

Joint Committees Exemplify Shared Administration Vision

TOLEDO, OHIO. The 2001-2004 agreement between the Toledo Federation of Teachers and the Toledo Public Schools describes a number of joint committees that are examples of shared administration.

- **School Intervention Teams.** The agreement creates the right for individual schools to establish joint School Intervention Teams that shall have the responsibility for "the improvement of a school's operation." Any such team must prepare guidelines for changes and monitor the results.[16]

- **Curriculum Committees.** The agreement states that teachers shall serve on all committees relating to curriculum, testing, and staff/professional development. A joint curriculum committee must be established with the authority to "make recommendations with respect to instructional programs or committee work." The Curriculum Committee must review any new curricular programs before they are submitted to the board.[17]

- **Professional Development Committee.** The agreement requires that a joint Professional Development Committee be established to review coursework and other professional development activities completed by teachers for the renewal of certificates and/or licenses. The committee is also charged to review and approve all coursework and workshops that count toward certification and/or licensure. Four of its six members are to be teachers, appointed by the union. The chair must

also be a teacher and shall be released full time from teaching duties "when full funding is available through the Ohio Department of Education."[18]

- **Professional Development Academy.** The agreement requires that the board and the union jointly develop and present a Professional Development Academy offering programs for new and more experienced teachers. Within parameters stated in the agreement, content decisions are to be made jointly by the board and the federation.[19]

CASE EXAMPLE:

Teacher Feedback Mandated On Variety of Learning Decisions

ROCHESTER, N.Y. The 2002 agreement between the City School District of Rochester and the Rochester Teachers Union requires that all administrative proposals involving school groupings and department groupings, new curriculum, in-service programs, and the selection of textbooks and materials be reported to teachers on the appropriate staff "for their ideas and suggestions." Feedback from the teachers must be considered by the administration in deciding whether to implement the new proposals. Further, teachers are given the right to initiate discussions about the same matters, instead of waiting for administrative proposals.[20]

CASE EXAMPLE:

Issues Committee Is One Outcome Of 1987 Strike in Wash. State

EDMONDS, WASH. After a bitter 30-day strike in 1987, the Edmonds School District and Edmonds Education Association worked with a consultant to establish a Labor Management Issues Committee (LMI). Over the following few years, the LMI oversaw the implementation of site-based decision-making. There is a partnership between principals and building representatives who meet as often as daily to do problem-solving and planning, if conditions warrant. The building reps have release time to do this work. Monthly, the "administrative cabinet" and union officers meet for long-range planning and problem-solving. The parties jointly publish an *Association/District Agreement Notebook*, which includes all joint implementation memos.

As the relationship matured, the parties institutionalized the *Agreement Notebook* in a Trust Agreement that guides further work.

CASE EXAMPLE:

Shrinking District in Michigan Turns to Far-Reaching Team Strategy

TAYLOR, MICH. Two institutionalized labor-management partnership structures are at work in the Taylor School District. Taylor is a small suburb near Detroit that, for years, has experienced a declining job market and a shrinking student-age population. The district currently has a student population of roughly 10,000, down from 26,000 during the 1960s and 1970s. Financial resources decline with enrollment because Michigan is a 'choice state' and public education dollars are attached to individual students. As students leave the district, so does the money.[21]

The partnerships in Taylor are the Labor Management Committee, and a much larger and further-reaching District Vertical Team. The Labor Management Committee is a joint standing committee with a membership that includes administrators, school board members, and union presidents (not only teachers).[22]

The District Vertical Team is more integral to the governance of the district, more active, and more fluid. It is organized into five active committees, comprised of between 40 and 60 people at any given time, including district central

staff, principals, teachers, clerical staff, and maintenance workers. The committees are focused on specific areas of operations, such as finance and enrollment, marketing, financial efficiencies, historical development, and budget development. From time to time, they are assigned specific tasks by the superintendent, at which point they break off into groups to do their work. Frequently, the entire Vertical Team meets together to learn about a particular issue or hear a speaker. Members are taught the basics of budget management and accounting; they may hear from the mayor about matters of local concern.

An example of a Vertical Team committee initiative is a marketing campaign that was developed in the summer of 2003. Because Michigan families have a high degree of choice in school selection, marketing can make a large difference in enrollment and tuition revenue. In an effort to reverse enrollment declines in the 2003-2004 school year, the committee created and coordinated a series of newspaper, television, and radio ads with representatives of labor and management, along with other constituencies, emphasizing the considerable strengths of the district. The result was 200 additional enrollees.[23]

CASE EXAMPLE:

District/Union Partnership Prints Restructuring Handbook

ALBUQUERQUE, N.MEX. After tense contract negotiations in 1988, the Albuquerque Teachers Federation and the Albuquerque Public Schools began to use Interest Based Bargaining in 1989. Since that time, the parties have agreed on the election of high school department chairs and later, elected chairs of lower grades. School Restructuring Councils were established as site decision-making bodies at the school level, and the district/union partnership published the Restructuring Handbook. The Sick Leave Bank became a self-funded, employee-owned entity. The district provides technical assistance to the Sick Leave Bank in administering the benefits.

Recently, the School Restructuring Councils evolved into school-level Instructional Councils (IC). The Instructional Councils are focused on instructional improvements and are comprised of administrators, teachers, and parents, elected to the councils.

OTHER DISTRICTS WITH STRATEGIC PARTNERSHIPS:

- Belleville, Ill.
- Denver
- New Orleans
- St. Paul, Minn.

CONTRACT LANGUAGE EXAMPLES

2003-2006 Collective Bargaining Agreement between the Boston Teachers Union and the Boston School Committee. Article III, Section C.

SHARED DECISION MAKING
Operation of the School Site Council
The parties expect the members of a school site council to operate as a single decision-making team, not as a group of spokespersons representing constituent groups. Their role is to work together to find good solutions to educational problems confronting the school. Members are chosen from various groups to insure that decisions reflect the expertise and input of important affected groups.

2001-2004 Agreement between Toledo Federation of Teachers and Toledo Public Schools. Article XXV; Article XXVI A.

SCHOOL INTERVENTION TEAM
Upon mutual agreement of the Superintendent and Federation, a joint team appointed by the parties shall be given responsibility for the improvement of a school's operation. The team will construct guidelines for changes and monitor the results.

DEVELOPMENT OF INSTRUCTIONAL PROGRAMS-COMMITTEES
Teachers shall serve on all committees relating to curriculum, testing and staff/professional development...Teacher appointments shall be made by the Federation...A curriculum committee shall be established composed of eight (8) members, four (4) each appointed by the Federation and the Board...

Trust Agreement Between the Edmonds School District and the Edmonds Education Association.

III. Mutual Interests
The Association and the District are committed to achieving the following mutual interests:
A. Support for the District Mission and Goals. The District's mission was developed through the combined interaction of community members and staff. It acknowledges the importance of maximizing the personal, creative and academic potential of each person in the school system. We commit to operating in ways which help realize this mission for all learners.

B. Accountability for Quality and Performance. We commit to improving existing structures to increase the accountability of those participating in the school system. Teachers, students and parents share accountability for student performance, and the community is accountable for making available the resources needed to meet the learning needs of its families and its children.

C. Solvency...
D. Professionalization of Teaching and Teaching Support...
E. Shared Decision Making...

Continued on Page 124

Continued from Page 123

F. Individual Rights and Responsibilities…
G. Parent and Community Involvement…

The Negotiated Agreement Between the Board of Education of the Albuquerque Municipal School District Number 12 and the Albuquerque Teachers Federation, 2002-2004.

Article 1
D. Instructional Councils (IC)
The District and the Federation agree to support the work of each school's Instructional Council (IC). ICs are established as part of a collaborative effort to improve and support the teaching and learning process in the Albuquerque Public Schools.

It is the intent of the District and the Federation to allow the individuals on each council to use their collective expertise and experience concerning their site and community to address school issues that fall within the scope of instructional improvement. The following requirements and recommendations set limited parameters.

The IC includes the Principal, a Federation representative selected by Federation members at the school, teachers elected by teachers, and parents representative of the school parent body, and may include representatives of other bargaining units as defined in their respective negotiated agreements, and any other personnel and/or students deemed appropriate by the IC and elected by their constituent group.

Teachers shall comprise at least fifty percent (50%) of the IC.

Meetings shall be open to any member of the school staff or school community.

The IC shall comply with Negotiated Agreements, Board policies, District procedures/directives, New Mexico laws/regulations and Federal laws/regulations when addressing issues. Issues shall be addressed in a collaborative manner.

Specific structure and protocol for the IC shall be developed by the IC and published for the school community.

If a decision concerning an issue cannot be reached by the IC, the Principal retains the right to make a decision if one has to be made.*

IC members have certain obligations, rights and responsibilities of membership, including attending and actively participating on the IC; reaching out to the diversity of the represented group to hear their opinions and ideas; communicating those opinions to the IC; supporting goals and strategies to implement the school's improvement plan; and collectively supporting the school improvement process.

IC Development. IC members should receive training to build capacity of the group in the concepts and skills of joint problem solving, team building and teamwork, parental involvement and decision making.

ICs may desire team facilitation or development services from time to time and may access joint training and facilitation support services from the Federation and the District. Requests for training and/or facilitation support services shall be made by the Chairperson of the IC to the District's Labor Relations Director and/or the Federation President.

Amended, 2004
The principal will support decisions made by the IC, when such decisions are reached in accordance with Article 1, section D5. There is an expectation that the principals and staff work together.

RESOURCES AND REFERENCES

- **Board of Education of the Albuquerque Municipal School District Number 12**
Rita Siegel, Labor Relations Board of Education
725 University Blvd., SE, Albuquerque, NM 87125
Tel: 505.842.3524

- **Albuquerque Teachers Federation**
Ellen Bernstein, President
8009 Mountain Road Place, NE Albuquerque, NM 87110
Tel: 505.262.2657   Fax: 505-266-1967
www.aftunion.org

- **Boston Teachers Union**
Richard Stutman, President
180 Mt. Vernon Street Boston, MA 02125
Tel: 617.BTU.2000
www.btu.org
rstutman@btu.org

- **Boston Public Schools**
Thomas Payzant, Superintendent
26 Court Street, Boston, MA 02108
Tel: 617.635.9050
www.boston.k12.ma.us

- **Edmonds Public Schools**
Jane Westergaard-Nimock, Director
20420 68th Ave. West, Lynnwood, WA 98036-7400
Tel: 425.670.7000

- **Edmonds Education Association**
Dan Wilson, President
19707 64th Ave. W., Suite 204, Lynnwood, WA 98036
Tel: 425.774.8851

- **Rochester Public Schools**
Manuel J. Rivera
Superintendent Rochester Public Schools
131 West Broad Street, Rochester, NY 14614
Tel: 585.262 8100
www.rcsdk12.org
manuel.rivera@rcsdk12.org

- **Rochester Teachers Association**
Adam Urbanski, President
Rochester Teachers Association
30 N. Union Street, Suite 301, Rochester, NY 14607
Tel: 585.546.2681
www.rochesterteachers.com
urbanski@rochesterteachers.com

- **Taylor Public Schools**
James Harris, Superintendent
23033 Northline Road, Taylor, MI 48180
Tel: 734.374.1206
www.taylorschools.net

- **Taylor Federation of Teachers**
Nancy Myers, President
Taylor Federation of Teachers, Local 1085 AFL-CIO
22770 Northline Road, Taylor, MI 48180
Tel: 734.287.3340
www.tft1085.org

- **Toledo Public Schools**
Eugene T.W. Sanders, Superintendent
420 E. Manhattan Boulevard, Toledo, OH 43608
Tel: 419.729.8200

- **Toledo Federation of Teachers**
Francine Lawrence, President
111 S. Byrne Road, Toledo, OH 43615
Tel: 419.535.3013
www.tft250.org

CHAPTER FOOTNOTES

1. Research shows us that diverse problem-solving groups are more creative and find better solutions than groups of people with like backgrounds, skills, or positions. To see more: James Surowiecki. 2004. *The Wisdom of Crowds.* New York: Doubleday.

2. An interesting example is the Delaware legislature's decision to implement teacher accountability tied to student test scores. The prototype must be piloted in several districts, but the Delaware State Education Association has stated that it will not participate. As a result, unionized districts are not willing to violate their collective-bargaining agreements to volunteer for the pilot. Delaware Secretary of Education Valerie Woodruff said: "One might call it a stalemate." Michele Fuetsch. "Pilot Plan to Evaluate Teachers OK'd." *The New Journal.* Aug. 14, 2004.

3. Robert B. Leventhal. 1991."What Managers Should Know about Union Involvement in New Work Systems." *Journal of Quality and Participation.* June 1991.

4. John R. Hibbing and Elizabeth Theiss-Morse. 2002. *Americans' Beliefs About How Government Should Work.* New York: Cambridge University Press.

5. Robert Klitgaard and Gregory F. Treverton. March 2003. *Assessing Partnerships: New Forms of Collaboration.* IBM Center for the Business of Government. www.businessofgovernment.org

6. Robert Evans. 1995. *The Human Side of School Change.* San Francisco: Jossey-Bass. Page 36.

7. Richard Elmore, 2002. *Bridging the Gap Between Standards and Achievement: The Imperative for Professional Development in Education.* Washington, D.C. The Albert Shanker Institute. www.ashankerinst.org

8. If not for the existence of public school systems there are no teachers' unions; without the cooperation of teachers and their unions, there may be fewer public schools or districts. Barbara Gray. 1989. *Collaborating: Finding Common Ground for Multiparty Problems.* San Francisco: Jossey-Bass.

9. Charles T. Kerchner, Julia E. Koppich, and Joseph G. Weeres. 1997. *United Mind Workers: Unions and Teaching in the Knowledge Society.* San Francisco: Jossey-Bass. Pp. 44-45.

10. For schematics of different governance arrangements, see Andy Banks and Jack Metzgar. "Participating in Management." 1989. *Labor Research Review.* Vol. 14.

11. Thomas A. Kochan, Harry C. Katz, and Robert B. McKersie. 1986. *The Transformation of American Industrial Relations.* New York: Basic Books. Page 179.

12. 2002-2005 Agreement and Partnership Between School District No. 1 in the City and County of Denver, State of Colorado and Denver Classroom Teachers Association. APPENDIX A. Page 74.

13. Ibid. Article II, Sec. B. 2.

14. Ibid, Article II, Sec. 3.

15. Ibid. Article III Sec. C-2.

16. 2001-2004 Agreement Between the Toledo Federation of Teachers and Toledo Public Schools. Article XXV.

17. Ibid. Article XXVI.

18. Ibid. Article XXVIII.

19. Ibid. Article XXVIII, Sec. D.

20. July 1, 2002, Agreement between the City School District of Rochester and Rochester Teachers Association. Section 27-1.

21. November 2004 telephone interviews with Nancy Myers, union president, and James Harris, superintendent, Taylor, Mich.

22. There are five unions in the district, one of which is the teachers' union. All are represented on the Labor Management Committee.

23. November 2004 telephone interviews with Nancy Meyers, union president.

JOINT PROBLEM-SOLVING

Joint problem-solving refers to mechanisms that allow district and union representatives to identify and address issues of mutual concern regarding improving student achievement. Joint problem-solving often results in the development of more formalized strategic partnerships and can be considered on the same evolutionary continuum. Joint problem-solving, as defined in this section, has little to do with grievances or individualized complaints. With joint problem-solving, parties contribute their perspectives and combine their resources to improve outcomes. Predictably, the parties often have different interests in a problem and/or its solution, but they come together over their mutual desire to have it resolved satisfactorily.

USEFULNESS TO IMPROVING STUDENT ACHIEVEMENT

Joint problem-solving addresses policies and procedures that are perceived by one side or both as obstacles to meeting accountability targets. Usually, district and union representatives from the same district work together on specific issues. Success is defined in various ways and centered on improved student outcomes. Involvement in joint problem-solving makes it more likely that the right resources are working on the problem and that individuals who are engaged in the change process will feel ownership in new practices and have confidence in adopting them.

Despite the high payoff potential of involving teachers in joint problem-solving related to issues of practice, there are several cautions to keep in mind. The first is that if teachers are invited to participate, then their participation must be meaningful and include the ability to influence decisions and policies. Too often, the "rhetoric" of participation does not meet the "reality."[24] The second is that participation and collegiality are hard to achieve.[25] Joint problem-solving efforts are fragile, hard to start, and hard to sustain. After all, they are addressing entrenched problems, and joint activities and problem-solving are both contrary to the norms of the organization. Despite the fact that many teachers want to participate, others will resist engagement because of the time and effort required and because isolation has its benefits: autonomy.[26] Administrators may be ambivalent because this work may seem like it is diminishing their power. It helps all parties if effort is not only supported but also modeled by the leaders at the top of the organization.

Joint problem-solving can take many forms along a continuum of formality and structure. In some districts, important joint problem-solving initiatives exist in the form of intentional informal working relationships between union and management leaders. Casual and informal (though not necessarily unplanned) conversations are very often the beginning of problem-solving.[27] Formal joint problem-solving processes that are organized around specific strategic issues represent the alternative extreme.[28] These processes may be governed at the district level where joint *ad hoc* committees are authorized or at the building level where problem-solving committees exist.[29]

Studies of successful organizations show that performance improves when the people who work in the organization are involved in influencing their jobs and work setting, particularly in identifying and solving the problems of the organization.[30] The closer these processes are to the actual work, the better. In public school districts, high-involvement requires sharing information, investing in teachers' ability to work on problems related to practice, expanding their discretion and influence in the processes of defining problems, analyzing root causes, and seeking or designing solutions.

A common culture is created when professionals engage in long-term efforts to improve practice. This culture carries the norms and values of professional standards and continuous inquiry and learning[31] and serves to shape the behavior of the professionals.

CASE EXAMPLE:

Union President, Superintendent Meet Regularly To Talk Business

ABC CERRITOS, CALIF. ABC Cerritos is a district of 24,000 students next to Los Angeles. The superintendent and the union president in this district have formed a loose working relationship focused on reform. There is no reference to this informal problem-solving mechanism in the collective-bargaining agreement, nor any written description of what it is or how it works. Nevertheless, this joint problem-solving process has had a powerful impact on student achievement in this district—the gap in reading as measured by the California assessment test has narrowed as a result of joint union-management selection and implementation of the new reading programs.

The partnership began when the newly hired superintendent and union president began meeting privately every two weeks to focus on one problem and a few points of agreement. The superintendent and union president agreed that there was a pocket of obvious neglect in the district, a geographic area on the south side of Cerritos where student outcomes were particularly poor. They also concurred that reading proficiency was essential to student success and that the

American Federation of Teachers (AFT) had research-based information that might be helpful in developing a reading skill strategy for improving student outcomes. Neither the superintendent nor the union president wanted to waste time reinventing a wheel, so they agreed to start working on their issues by reviewing relevant AFT-generated material and considering how it might apply to their particular situation.

The superintendent and union president began meeting bi-weekly. Besides their central issue, they discussed other matters of mutual concern, including teacher compensation, district finances, and employee healthcare. While there was nothing surreptitious about their meetings, they consciously chose not to institutionalize the process by creating a policy or language in their contract or any form of memorandum. They wanted to stay low-key and flexible.

In addressing the poor performance of the district's South Side schools, the superintendent and president agreed upon a joint study tour, using a protocol designed by the AFT. They authorized a team of teachers and administrators to tour other districts using several recommended research-based reading programs. They wanted to learn about the strengths and weaknesses of a variety of programs and then make recommendations to their constituents. Ultimately, teachers were given the opportunity to vote by secret ballot on the program that should be adopted in their building. If the vote was not unanimous, discussion was re-opened; the merits and weaknesses of programs were further investigated, and the secret vote was repeated.

To be sure, there are skeptics in the union in ABC Cerritos who feel that the "relationship" between the president and the superintendent is too cozy. Clearly, it would not be tolerated were either the administration or the union to perceive that their interests were being compromised because of it. However, it appears that the opposite is true, and that the partnership is serving the interests of both parties well. While the union and the administration have not stopped disagreeing,

they disagree less frequently and disruptively. There are fewer grievances overall, and more grievances are settled at lower levels in the grievance process. Contract negotiations have produced reasonable salary increases for teachers, and favorable benefit packages have been retained. The union has remained very active politically and is a strong force in school board elections.

Significantly, the informal relationship between the superintendent and the union president is now spilling over into other departments and to the building level. Annually, the district, union, and building leaders participate in a retreat that includes briefings on finances and accountability. Building representatives are meeting with principals on a regular basis, and union officers in charge of employment issues are meeting with district department heads for human resources and curriculum. A culture of collaboration is developing, making way for specific initiatives and reforms. For example, the union and district have jointly collaborated in "shamelessly raiding other districts" for qualified teachers. An annual recruitment fair hosted by the union now attracts hundreds more qualified teacher candidates than the district can hire.[32]

CASE EXAMPLE:

Continuous Improvement Key In Growing Colo. District

DOUGLAS COUNTY SCHOOL DISTRICT, COLO. Douglas County is a fast-growing southern suburb of Denver. This district and AFT Local 2265 have established a strategic partnership that has lasted for over a decade. The experience of working together in this partnership has also provided a foundation for more widespread joint problem-solving work, which has now been institutionalized over a long period of time. Joint problem-solving has been incorporated and utilized regularly throughout the system,

EXAMPLES OF CONTRACT LANGUAGE

**From the Douglas County Public Schools
Web Site: www1.dcsdk12.org**

The agenda for the Cabinet meetings are set in advance in order to maximize efficiency and to follow a quality model. The agenda is made up of topics and recommendations submitted by cabinet members and are structured in the following format:

I. TOPIC - An issue that needs attention is presented to the cabinet.

II. RECOMMENDATIONS - The person(s) presenting the issue must also have possible solutions prepared.

III. FEEDBACK - Cabinet discusses the recommendations presented.

IV. DECISION - Cabinet may approve a recommendation, or request additional work be done regarding the issue.

The Cabinet serves as a strategic sounding board and, when necessary, a decision-making body for the Superintendent. Whenever possible, though, the group wants to communicate its efforts broadly and to drive decision-making to the appropriate level in the organization.

The primary monitoring of the three strategic directions—Student Achievement, Effective Use of Resources and Responsive Governance—occurs through the work of the designated Project Team Leaders, each of whom serves on Cabinet. The Goals and Executive Limitations found within the Board's Policy Governance book drive the work of the Superintendent's Cabinet.

reinforcing the strong working relationship of the union and district management.[33]

The Douglas County School District uses continuous improvement strategies, as outlined in the Baldridge Program. Project teams are formed to work on specific problems in the system under a charter approved by the superintendent's cabinet. A problem is identified and presented to the cabinet. The members then decide if the issue warrants a multi-stakeholder project team. If they conclude that it does, a charter is issued for a team. The charter includes a statement about the performance shortfall to be addressed, the names of stakeholders nominated for membership on the project team, a projection of the benefits of improving performance, and a timeline for completing the project, including a report to the cabinet. The project team looks at root causes of problems using quality/continuous improvement techniques such as "fishbone diagrams" and variations of statistical process control. Possible solutions are also examined using techniques such as "benchmarking." The project team solicits feedback on the suggested solutions from stakeholder groups. After a presentation to the cabinet, the team may be given permission to implement a solution and monitor results.

The following excerpt from a project team charter provides an example of a problem brought before the cabinet:

> The district does not have a comprehensive instructional program that utilizes research based best practices, is aligned with the District's evaluation system and includes a systematic K-12 intervention/remediation program for literacy.

An initial report to the cabinet included an analysis of the district's instructional practices and areas of the misalignment between the programs, best practices, the districts' teacher evaluation system, and remediation programs. The conclusion was that the district had adopted a hodgepodge of intervention/remediation programs rather than one program and had not required that the programs be 'research-based.' The project team made several recommendations for actions on a grade-by-grade level.

OTHER EXAMPLES OF DISTRICTS USING JOINT PROBLEM-SOLVING:

- Albuquerque, N.Mex.
- Brevard County, Fla.
- Cleveland
- Collier County, Fla.
- New Orleans
- Palm Beach, Fla.
- Perth Amboy, N.J.
- Rochester, N.Y.
- San Francisco
- Seattle

RESOURCES AND REFERENCES

- **ABC Cerritos Teachers Association**
  Laura Rico, President
  12028 Centralia Road, Suite 204,
  Hawaiian Gardens, CA 90716
  Tel: 562.942.6942

- **ABC Unified School District**
  Ronald Barnes, Superintendent
  16700 Norwalk Boulevard, Cerritos, CA 90703
  Tel: 562.926.5566
  www.abcusd.k12.ca.us

- **Douglas County Federation of Teachers**
  Pat McGraw, President
  422 Elbert Street, Castle Rock, Colorado 80104
  Tel: 303.688.3381   Fax: 303-688-1039
  www.dcft.net

- **Douglas County School District**
  Jim Christensen, Superintendent
  620 Wilcox Street, Castle Rock, Colorado 80104
  Tel: 303.387.0123   Fax: 303-387-0107
  www1.dcsdk12.org

CHAPTER FOOTNOTES

24. Barbara Turnbull. 2003. "Research Note: Shared Decision Making-Rhetoric Versus Reality." *Journal of School Leadership*. Volume 13:569-59.

25. Robert Evans. 1996. *The Human Side of School Change*. San Francisco: Jossey-Bass. Pp. 234-241.

26. Nearly 90 percent of teachers report that they are "very" or "somewhat" interested in "having more influence and getting more involved in decisions over curriculum and instruction." Public Agenda Foundation. 2003. *Stand by Me: What Teachers Think About Unions, Merit Pay and Other Professional Matters*. www.publicagenda.org

27. ABC Cerritos, Calif., is an example.

28. Chicago is an example.

29. For more on this, see Allyne Beach and Linda Kaboolian, *Public Service, Public Savings: Case Studies in Labor Management Efforts to Improve the Public Sector*. June 2003. Ford Foundation. www.pslmc.org

30. Edward E. Lawler III. 1986. *High-involvement Management: Participative Strategies for Improving Organizational Performance*. San Francisco: Jossey-Bass.

31. Wilbur Brookover. 1982. *Creating Effective Schools: An In-Service Program for Enhancing School Learning Climate and Achievement*. Holmes Beach, Fla.: Learning Publications.

32. Much of the information in this section was obtained in a telephone interview with Laura Rico, union president, on Nov. 17, 2003.

33. The strength of this collaborative working relationship is evident in multiple ways. The union is part of the superintendent's cabinet. The school board invited the union to play a formal role in the search for the current superintendent. The parties work together on virtually every aspect of education reform.

EXTERNAL PARTNERSHIPS

External partnerships are typically joint working relationships between different stakeholders. Through these partnerships, different agencies are able to combine resources and bring broad perspective and common focus to school improvement efforts.

External partnerships exist in various forms, ranging from inter-district networks of labor and management teams that are experiencing similar challenges, to wider-reaching, multi-party coalitions that might include school districts, teachers' unions, and important constituencies such as business, education, community stakeholders, and others.

USEFULNESS TO IMPROVING STUDENT ACHIEVEMENT

Partnerships between and among unions, districts, and universities (typically graduate schools of education) are especially well suited to focus on strategies for improving student achievement. Partnerships often focus on teacher training, teacher recruitment, data collection, data analysis, curriculum development, and more.

External partnerships address problems caused by capacity limitations, as well as allaying public concerns about the legitimacy of reform innovations undertaken by the school district. They also serve to generate new ideas and solutions through a sharing of perspectives. In this way, external partnerships reduce the isolation that many education professionals experience.

CASE EXAMPLE:

Cleveland Academy Targets Teachers' Professional Growth

CLEVELAND. The Cleveland Teachers Academy (CTA) is a partnership of the Cleveland Teachers Union, the Cleveland Municipal School District, the Cleveland Initiative for Education, and several universities.[34] Its purpose is "to create a teacher renewal process that serves as a catalyst for professional growth opportunities" necessary for accomplished teaching and improved student achievement. The CTA was created in 1996 to supplement professional development opportunities already available to teachers in the district. Member teachers of CTA design and implement courses and other initiatives designed to improve instruction and drive better student outcomes. The union president and the superintendent co-chair the Academy. Board members include other senior union officers, as well as representatives from Baldwin-Wallace College, John Carroll University, Cleveland State University, and the George Gund Foundation.[35]

CTA's implementation was originally scheduled for three years (commencing in 2002). Nine schools (of the district's 125) participated in year one, 18 schools in year two, and 36 schools in year three. The original nine schools were voluntary participants considered to already have positive labor-management relations. Labor and management representatives from this first cohort worked together to learn from one another. They participated in three retreats and many inter-school activities designed to highlight, share, and capture the best teaching practices in each. School-based and district-wide leadership teams were formed from within the group of nine schools. In year two, a second cohort of nine schools joined the initiative as mentees, to participate in activities designed to build on the first year's learning, as well as to affirm, develop,

and refine successes observed. Models were developed to be disseminated further throughout the district, specifically through 18 more schools added in year three.[36]

Current CTA initiatives include the following:

- Creating small learning communities within high schools
- Building an AFT Reading Project through joint efforts of the union and district
- Training facilitators to work within individual schools on strategic annual academic plans
- Supporting teacher candidates for National Board Professional Teaching status
- Facilitating the creation of teacher study groups and summer study opportunity
- Offering innovative methods training to teachers for literacy programs, and
- Offering exposure to local and national experts addressing literacy issues[37]

Because of CTA, the union and the district in Cleveland received the 2001 Saturn/UAW Award sponsored by the American Federation of Teachers and Saturn to recognize outstanding labor-management collaboration efforts to improve teacher performance and improve public education.[38]

There is no reference to CTA in the 2000-2003 collective-bargaining agreement.

CASE EXAMPLE:

Experimental Arts Program Eyed as Inspiration for Change

MINNEAPOLIS. The *Arts for Academic Achievement* program in Minneapolis represents a significant external partnership, enabling flexibility between the union and district management on issues related to collaboration and student-focused innovation.

EXAMPLES OF CONTRACT LANGUAGE:

**CTA Mission Statement
(not in collective bargaining agreement):**

The Cleveland Teachers Academy's purpose is to create a teacher renewal process that serves as a catalyst for professional growth opportunities needed to become more accomplished practitioners. CTA is the challenger of teachers to serve effectively as school-wide change leaders.

The mission statement and more information on The Cleveland Teachers Academy is available on the Web at www.ci4edu.org.

2003-2005 Agreement between the Minneapolis Board of Education and the Minneapolis Federation of Teachers. Article 5.

Standards: Teacher induction/development programs must be a collaboration between district(s) and colleges/universities in program design to:

- Address the needs of the District Improvement Agenda.
- Incorporate a professional development process to support its participants.
- Develop, in collaboration with the district, a process to measure the effectiveness of the teacher training programs, and report results annually to the Teacher Development Council.

Arts for Academic Achievement is a partnership formed by the Minneapolis Public Schools and the Perpich Center for Arts Education. It has received a $3.2 million challenge grant from the Annenberg Foundation to design an innovative curriculum that will integrate arts and non-arts disciplines in order to increase learning in the non-arts subjects.[39] The success of *Arts for Academic Achievement* requires labor and management in the Minneapolis school district to be partners in joint efforts of internal instructional innovation.

Arts for Academic Achievement starts in schools where a team of teachers designs a program that brings artists and arts organizations into the teaching and learning processes. School-based programs must be linked to school and school district improvement plans. Conformity among schools is not required, however, or even encouraged. The project is experimental, such that schools themselves become laboratories for instructional innovation. Accordingly, work rules are implicated in a variety of ways and in a variety of settings. To succeed, teachers and

administrators must be flexible with one another in managing modified day-to-day operations.

There is no reference to *Arts for Academic Achievement* in the collective-bargaining agreement.

OTHER EXAMPLES OF DISTRICTS
WITH EXTERNAL PARTNERSHIPS:

- Cincinnati
- Montgomery County, Md.
- Seattle

- Demonstrate program success indicated by a completion rate of at least 60% and its participants passing the PPST.
- Demonstrate that its participants are working towards achieving the ten national Interstate New Teacher Assessment and Support Consortium (INTASC) standards.
- Provide placement of participants with cooperating/supervising teachers who model the Standards of Effective Instruction.
- Articulate a program design that includes: field experience, job embedded staff development, instruction, continuous assessment, supervision, due process, and adequate funding and adjunct status for Minneapolis teachers.

CHAPTER FOOTNOTES

34. The Cleveland Initiative for Education (CIE) is a nonprofit organization established in 1990 by business and philanthropic leaders in Cleveland to foster and support reform in the schools. The CTA is one of CIE's several programs, each of which strategically engages the local business community in efforts to strengthen the Cleveland Public School System.

35. Piet van Lier. May/June 2000 online issue of Catalyst For Cleveland Schools. Also, PSLMC Case Studies. www.pslmc.org/casestudies.asp?caseID=10. Accessed Jan. 15, 2004.

36. PSLMC Case Study, Page 2. A.

37. Appendix B: Visit Report—Cleveland. http://search.netscape.com/ns/boomerang.jsp?query=clev

38. PSLMC Case Study, Page 3.

39. http://education.umn.edu/CAREI/Reports/default.html

RESOURCES AND REFERENCES

- **Cleveland Teachers Union**
  Michael Charney, Professional Issues Director
  1370 West 6th Street, 4th Floor, Cleveland, OH 44113
  Tel: 216.861.7676, ext. 239   Fax: 216-861-4113

- **Cleveland Municipal School District**
  Barbara Byrd-Bennett, Superintendent
  1380 East 6th Street, Cleveland, OH 44114
  Tel: 216.574.8000

- **Minneapolis Public Schools**
  Patricia Thornton, Coordinator
  159 Pillsbury Drive SE, Minneapolis, MN 55455
  Tel: 612.625.8974 Fax: 612.624.8744

- **College-School Collaborations in Teacher Development**
  Minneapolis Public Schools
  159 Pillsbury Drive SE, Minneapolis, MN 55455
  Tel: 612.625.8974   Fax: 612.624.8744
  kalni001@tc.umn.edu

- **Minneapolis Federation of Teachers**
  Louise Sundin, President
  67 8th Avenue, NE, Minneapolis, MN 55413
  Tel: 612.529.9621
  www.MFT59.org

CROSS-DISTRICT ADVOCACY COALITIONS

Cross-district advocacy coalitions stimulate inter-district collaboration for purposes of improving performance results. While not strictly an innovation involving a collective-bargaining contract, this partnership form is of such significance that it bears inclusion in this handbook.

Coalitions, like the example described below, allow districts to speak with a unified voice to the public, legislature, and the state department of education about policies that affect education reform, including finance, assessments, and teacher quality.

USEFULNESS TO IMPROVING STUDENT ACHIEVEMENT

Cross-district coalitions can offer mutual benefits on many levels, including academic, technical, financial, and political. The unity of the coalition means that differences between the parties are not exploitable.

The Ohio 8 Coalition is a powerful and unique political force that has created a unified labor and management voice to inform, advocate, and influence policy and practice involving public education reform in the state of Ohio.[40] National observers believe it is the only organization of its type in the nation.[41] The Coalition is a strategic alliance composed of the superintendents and teachers' union presidents from Ohio's eight largest urban school districts: Akron, Canton, Cincinnati, Cleveland, Columbus, Dayton, Toledo, and Youngstown. Member districts account for approximately one-sixth of Ohio's 1.8 million public school students. Nearly two-thirds of the students in the eight districts belong to a minority group.[42]

The Coalition was first convened in 2001 by four Ohio foundations—the Cleveland Foundation, the George Gund Foundation, the Martha Holden Jennings Foundation, and KnowledgeWorks.[43] It was founded on the principle that a high-performance public education system is essential to the civic and economic health of Ohio's cities. It places strong emphasis on the power of collaboration and partnership and works closely with legislators, educators, parents, labor, and community officials. The Coalition's primary strategy is to form a united front to influence state policy. While the Coalition was created for the specific purpose of influencing Ohio's Senate Bill 1 (a law designed to revamp the state's systems of academic standards and assessment), it has expanded its scope to include a range of education reform issues of particular interest to urban communities, including student performance, closing the achievement gap, school facilities, teacher quality, funding, public engagement, and implementation requirements of federal No Child Left Behind legislation. [44]

The Coalition has learned that when superintendents and union leaders are publicly united on education issues, they can send a powerful message to legislators and policymakers who do not expect the two sides to agree and who could otherwise exploit their differences. Members are convinced that when it comes to the future and success of public education, their common interests far outweigh their individual differences.

Besides providing a strong vehicle for external communication and influence with policymakers, the Coalition has fostered productive relationships between and among its members. Because there is more familiarity, trust, and understanding, districts share information and support one another on both the labor and management levels. Rather than adversaries, superintendents and union presidents present themselves as professional educators with common goals. Within districts, union leaders and administrators work more openly and with a higher level of respect for their different offices and perspectives.

The Coalition is governed by a Leadership Council, which is co-chaired by one superintendent and one union president selected from the eight member districts. [45] It has a part-time executive director who estimates that the job is half-time. [46] In all of the member districts combined, there are roughly 577 schools, 280,000 students, and 20,000 teachers. Each district is urban and relatively large. All but one district

have a majority of non-white students. The smallest district is Youngstown, with approximately 10,000 students and 730 teachers. Cleveland is the largest district, having about 72,000 students and nearly 6,500 teachers. [47] The Coalition's annual budget is about $300,000, which is funded by each member district and union, as well as five foundations, including the four founding foundations and the Joyce Foundation, which joined later.

The Coalition meets formally on a quarterly basis and sometimes more often. It maintains close contact with the state's top education policy authorities, including the state superintendent of education and staff of the governor's office. [48] One of the few rules of governance is that there shall be no substitute representatives at the meetings. If a member superintendent or union president is unable to attend a meeting, the absent member's chair remains empty. The rule is to reinforce the relationship-building component of the program, to stress the importance of a unified effort, and to maintain continuity. [49]

On a less formal level, Coalition members sometimes ask one another for help. Ideas, expertise, and even personnel have been shared. If one Coalition member district is struggling in a particular area, it might request another Coalition member district—known for having the best staff or practice or result—for assistance.

RESOURCES AND REFERENCES

■ **The Ohio 8 Coalition**
William Wendling , Executive Director
1422 Euclid Avenue, Suite 1530, Cleveland, OH 44115
Tel: 216.241.9400   Fax: 216.241.9425
www.catalyst-cleveland.org
bwendling@wendlingper.com

■ **KnowledgeWorks Foundation**
Harold Brown, School Improvement Program Officer
One W. 4th Street, Suite 200, Cincinnati, OH 45202
Tel: 513-929-4777   Fax: 513-929-1122
www.kwfdn.org
brownh@knfdn.org

CHAPTER FOOTNOTES

40. Much of the information in this summary is taken from the Ohio 8 Fact Sheet published by the Ohio 8 Coalition and provided by William Wendling, executive director of the Ohio 8.

41. The Ohio 8 Fact Sheet.

42. Stephens, Scott. Cleveland Plain Dealer. Dec. 1, 2002. Accessed from the Internet in October 2003.

43. KnowledgeWorks is a Cincinnati-based foundation which states as its vision a commitment to furthering universal access to high-quality educational opportunities. Information available on the Internet at www.kwfdn.org. At the time this book was researched, the Joyce Foundation was also providing additional funding.

44. Stephens, Scott. *Cleveland Plain Dealer*, Dec. 1, 2002. Accessed from the Internet in October 2003.

45. Currently the co-chairs are Barbara Byrd-Bennett, CEO of the Cleveland Municipal Schools, and John Grossman, president of the Columbus Education Association.

46. The executive director is William Wendling. Much information in this section was obtained in a telephone interview with Mr. Wendling on Nov. 15, 2003.

47. The Ohio Eight Fact Sheet, enrollment data. Taken from the Ohio Department of Education.

48. The state superintendent is Ohio's equivalent to another state's commissioner of education.

49. Stephens, Scott. Superintendents, Union Leaders Call A Truce and Align For Urban Education. *Cleveland Plain Dealer*, Dec. 1, 2002. Accessed from the Internet on Oct. 15, 2003.

Conclusion & Afterword
by the Rennie Center

The Rennie Center has produced this handbook in partnership with the book's researchers and authors— Linda Kaboolian and Paul Sutherland — to illustrate ways and means for improving the quality and effectiveness of labor-management relations in education.

As we indicated at the start of this reference guide, we hope that the innovations described here will not only inspire others, but will raise the field's expectations for *what is possible*—enabling district and union leaders to structure their own practices based on knowledge about other districts' accomplishments and innovative strategies for working together to improve student achievement. We reiterate that practices catalogued in this handbook are not prescriptions for change, but rather, possible models for simultaneously satisfying the institutional needs of negotiating parties and for improving student achievement.

There are no silver bullets or quick fixes to transform labor-management relations. However, a critical first step entails acknowledging that student learning should be at the core of professional relationships in public education. Recognizing this shared goal and adults' shared accountability for high levels of student performance provides a basis for collaboration and communication. It is the continual reiteration of this common purpose—rather than a desire to maintain smooth, conflict-free relations that only serve adult interests—that will keep professional relationships focused on a constructive, student-centered track.

Not all working relationships between district managers and teachers' union leaders begin with the same level of trust or collaborative spirit— some relationships have already resulted in advanced collaborative engagement; others are at the beginning stages of constructive relationship-building after turbulent histories. Each district's history, context, and relational experience are unique. Leaders' personalities and management styles are different. While the development of strong, trusting relationships is an important component of improving student achievement, the aim of this handbook is to encourage educational professionals to re-examine their existing working relationships in light of their capacity to improve student learning. It is our belief that a strong, explicit commitment to student achievement is the most promising response to the challenges of accountability and competition now confronting so many public school systems.

Collaboration on school reform is an evolving process—inevitably characterized by both successes and setbacks. Districts cited in case examples often initiated small, informal reform efforts and, as a base of experience developed, they grew their collaborative efforts to encompass more complex initiatives. Through this developmental process, both sides come to see collaboration as an opportunity to learn together. They take time to understand one another's motivations and needs. This gradual scaling of innovative practice also enables both sides to develop the necessary new skills required to work together at a leadership level, as well as to engage school-level constituencies in the process.

Labor-management experts provide the following additional advice on initiating meaningful collaborations between district management and teachers' union leaders:

- District management and teachers' union leaders should focus on improved student learning as the primary goal of their professional work together
- District management and teachers' union leaders need to recognize the other party(ies) as a legitimate actor(s) in educational reform with knowledge, insights, legitimate interests, and resources
- Effective collaboration entails that all participants clearly articulate expectations about the partnership and strive to create equitable roles
- Regular, explicit, and transparent communication is important between district management and teachers' union leadership
- The fact that both sides face risk in embarking on collaborative ventures should be remembered
- Labor and management leaders should involve each side from the start and focus on developing solutions that take each side's perspective into account
- District management and teachers' union leaders need to invest resources in the development of partners' capacity to work at higher levels

- Union and management collaborators should anticipate side benefits which may have overall value beyond their contribution to the immediate collaboration
- Both union and management leaders will have the incentive and obligation to focus on bigger-picture reform issues if collaboration is extended beyond trivial issues
- District management and teachers' union leadership should periodically evaluate the progress of their collaboration and adjust accordingly

There is no simple way to dramatically improve student achievement, let alone reform public education by improving the current state of labor-management relations. We remain convinced that dramatic improvement in labor-management collaboration is essential to realizing our national aspirations to provide all children with a high-quality education. This is high-risk, very sensitive, pioneering work that must be at the core of successful education reform. Issues of labor-management relations are commonly avoided in the policy, political, and practice communities for fear of arousing anxieties and hostilities and thereby creating problems. Leaders neglect current opportunities for constructive activism at their peril, thus allowing underlying problems to worsen, and the ultimate goal of improving student achievement to become more elusive. In these cases, the entire field suffers.

We encourage educational leaders to join us in addressing this situation head-on, dedicating the time, energy, resources, and public commitment necessary to make real change and develop the effective working relationships necessary to significantly boost student achievement and improve schools.

Acknowledgements

The Rennie Center would like to express our gratitude to the many individuals who helped with the creation of this book. First and foremost, this work would not be possible without the generous sponsorship of the Jessie B. Cox Charitable Trust and the Barr Foundation, as well as support from the Noyce Foundation and the Nellie Mae Education Foundation.

We feel fortunate to have worked with the book's researchers and authors, Linda Kaboolian and Paul Sutherland of the Public Sector Labor Management Program within the Taubman Center for State and Local Government at Harvard University's John F. Kennedy School of Government. A long-time expert on labor relations in the education sector, Linda brings decades of experience and insight on the topic. Her work on this book leverages her experience working on multi-stakeholder problem-solving processes in the workplace and history of engagement with labor and management groups on improving organizational performance. Paul Sutherland's contributions are informed by his work as an attorney with more than 20 years of experience in public school and municipal labor relations.

We also thank the book's reviewers, whose insight and commentary were invaluable in shaping this text, including: members of MassINC's research team, as well as Elizabeth Valerio, Deutsch Williams BD&H; Claudia Bach, Andover Public Schools; Michael Long, Long & Long; and Edward Doherty, Massachusetts Federation of Teachers.

We thank the many individuals working in districts cited within this handbook. We anticipate that the example set with these districts' innovation and dedication to student-centered decision-making will provide inspiration and models for educational leaders in districts across the nation. We are grateful for the time and effort that district leaders dedicated to this work, including interviews with the book's researchers and time spent reviewing case examples for accuracy.

The researchers' search was aided by the national teachers' associations, as well as organizations representing school boards, labor attorneys, and superintendents.

We recognize and thank our partners at Editorial Projects in Education for their support and guidance in publishing this text, especially, Virginia Edwards and her colleagues, Mary-Ellen Phelps Deily, Laura Baker, Vanessa Solis, Bob Rose, and Michele Givens.

With the production of this book, as well as with our larger labor-management initiative, we have benefited from the insights and expertise of a national, expert advisory board comprised of national and local representatives of teachers' unions, superintendents, school boards, policy leaders, business education activists, and labor relations experts. Members include:

Rosanne Bacon Meade, Co-Chair, Cambridge College; former President, Massachusetts Teachers Association

Peter Finn, *Co-Chair*, former Executive Director, Massachusetts Association of School Superintendents

Kathleen Kelley, President, Massachusetts Federation of Teachers

Irwin Blumer, Professor, Lynch School of Education, Boston College

Catherine Boudreau, President, Massachusetts Teachers Association

Sally Dias, Emmanuel College; former Superintendent of Watertown (Mass.) Public Schools

Edward Doherty, Massachusetts Federation of Teachers; former President of Boston Teachers Union

Roger Erskine, Teachers Union Reform Network, Seattle; former Executive Director, Seattle Education Association; former senior staffer, National Education Association

Thomas Hickey, South Shore Vocational School, Hanover, Mass., administrator and former teacher

David Hornbeck, President, International Youth Foundation; former Superintendent, Philadelphia Public Schools

Susan Moore Johnson, Professor, Harvard Graduate School of Education

Glenn Koocher, Executive Director, Massachusetts Association of School Committees

William McKersie, Associate Dean for Development and Alumni Affairs, Harvard Graduate School of Education

Thomas Scott, Executive Director, Massachusetts Association of School Superintendents; former Executive Director of EDCO Collaborative

Kathleen Skinner, Director, Massachusetts Teachers Association

Adam Urbanski, Founder and Director, Teachers Union Reform Network; President, Rochester (N.Y.) Teachers Association

Index